eet, 8 inches.

ight: 132

head:

high

brown

straight

small

small

brown

fair

small

arks: scar on right ear

PHOTO

Christian

STRATION CARD MUST BE CARRIED ON THE PERSON

**(PENALTY)**

An alien enemy required to register shall not, after the date fixed for his registration and the issuance to him of a registration card, be found within the limits of the United States, its territories or possessions, without having his registration card on his person under liability, among other penalties, to arrest and detention for the period of the war.

7—1102

ertifies

Oscar R Ba
(Name of registrant

residing at Ohio
(State.)

Alliance
(City, town.)

71 E Oxford
(Street and number.)

whose photograph and signature,

mark of identification, appear hereo

Ohio
(State.)

Alliance
(City, town.)

as a person required by law to register

mation of the President of the Uni

November 16, 1917.

Oscar R Bu

Alexander F. Barnes & Peter L. Belmonte

# FORGOTTEN SOLDIERS of WORLD WAR I

AMERICA'S

IMMIGRANT

DOUGHBOYS

Schiffer Publishing Ltd

4880 Lower Valley Road • Atglen, PA 19310

THIS BOOK IS DEDICATED TO THE FOREIGN-BORN
MEN AND WOMEN FROM MANY LANDS WHO
SERVED IN THE US MILITARY SO BRAVELY, SO LONG
AGO, IN THE GREAT WAR; DEMONSTRATING FOR
ALL TIME THAT AN AMERICAN IS ONE WHO IS
WILLING TO GIVE HIS LIFE FOR AMERICA.

*The magpies in Picardy*

*Are more than I can tell.*

*They flicker down the dusty roads*

*And cast a magic spell*

*On the men who march through Picardy,*

*Through Picardy to hell*


*He told me that in Picardy,*

*An age ago or more,*

*While all his fathers still were eggs,*

*These dusty highways bore*

*Brown singing soldiers marching out*

*Through Picardy to war.*


*T. P. Cameron Wilson*

*(Killed in action 23 March 1918)*

Designed by Molly Shields
Cover design by Matt Goodman

Type set in SackersGothicMedium/Times New Roman

ISBN: 978-0-7643-5547-9
Printed in China

Published by Schiffer Publishing, Ltd.
4880 Lower Valley Road
Atglen, PA 19310
Phone: (610) 593-1777; Fax: (610) 593-2002
E-mail: Info@schifferbooks.com
Web: www.schifferbooks.com

For our complete selection of fine books on this and related subjects, please visit our website at www.schiffer-
books.com. You may also write for a free catalog.

Schiffer Publishing's titles are available at special
discounts for bulk purchases for sales promotions or
premiums. Special editions, including personalized
covers, corporate imprints, and excerpts, can be
created in large quantities for special needs. For more
information, contact the publisher.

We are always looking for people to write books on
new and related subjects. If you have an idea for a book,
please contact us at proposals@schifferbooks.com.

# CONTENTS

# ACKNOWLEDGMENTS

Any work of this scope requires the help and support of many people. For the use of family photographs and other information: John Adams-Graf; Beverly Alexandria-Adamski; Cassandra Barnes; Reynaldo Cervantes Jr.; Ryan Conroy; the Cosentino family; Ruth Craig; Brennan Gauthier; Steve Girard; BG Marshall Kjelvik (VANG); Mark Koprcina; Jeffrey P. Magut, a valued member of the US Militaria forum; Rosemary Masters; Joel McConnell; Andrea Koprcina McGuire; Lori Berdak Miller; Carlton Moffatt; John E. Patton, our Hawaiian liaison officer; Lou Ponsi; Rose Presta Pennington; Kurt Rossi; Charles G. Thomas, another great US Militaria forum member; Christine Chiappetta Thorsen; Andrew Woods and J. Perkins at the First Division Museum at Cantigny, in Wheaton, Illinois; Mary Rockett and Gemma Rocchette; Bob Sartini; John Simmons; Vicky Zagame; the staff and crew at Advance Guard Militaria; and the Rhodes and Smergalski families.

There were also a number of people who lent their unique talents to helping us tell this story: Rogier van de Hoef, whose knowledge of the Dutch doughboys is unmatched; Ermalinda O. Dominguez, who cheerfully translated Pvt. Gonzales's writing; Gary Cieradkowski, who translated Polish documents; Walter Slonopas, who translated Russian material; John Halages and Bernadette Cornelius at Saints Constantine and Helen Greek Orthodox Cathedral in Richmond, Virginia, who translated the Greek; Bert J. Cunningham (historian, 69th Infantry Regiment, regimental headquarters) provided insight into the Rainbow Division; Chris Garcia of the Virginia War Museum lent his expertise on the 42nd Division in general and the 165th Infantry Regiment in particular; Carla Wieger, a world-class writer and Signal Corps officer, with her in-depth knowledge of the Hello Girls; Ms. Ann Calanni provided the story and pictures of her father, Salvatore (Sam) Calanni; Maj. (ret.) Richard Dell helped with the editing and sequence structure; Aaron Pollick, with his knowledge of the US military in the Hawaiian Islands; and Kevin Born, who helped make sure the pictures were the highest quality possible. The authors would like to thank Pete Schiffer and Bob Biondi for giving us the opportunity to tell this story, and also Ian Robertson for making it all work out so well.

To all of you, we say thank you; we truly hope we met your expectations.

And finally, to our wives, Michele Barnes and Pam Belmonte, who may not understand how we do this, but they do understand why.

All photographs and documents without credit lines in their captions are in private collections.

# FOREWORD
## *There's a Long, Long Trail A-winding . . .*

"Some of the best stuff of America has come out of foreign lands . . . and their belief in America has made them better citizens."[1] –Woodrow Wilson

One of the basic tenets in any successful military organization is the willingness to quickly obey orders given by a higher authority. But what happens when the receiver of the orders, although willing to obey, is unable to understand what he is being told to do? As the 305th Infantry Regiment of the 77th Division noted in their history:

> Imagine the difficulties of teaching the rudiments of military art to men, however willing, who couldn't understand; officers have had sometimes to get right down on their hands and knees to show by actual physical persuasion how to "advance and plant the left foot." Imagine, too, the difficulties of teaching . . . the methods of patrolling."[2]

The 305th Infantry Regiment and its higher command, the 77th Division, were admittedly a unique military unit, inasmuch as they were drawn from draftees from New York City, and their ranks included the ethnic and religious makeup of the city. It was written that the recruits reflected "all races and all creeds . . . Italians, Chinamen, the Jews and the Irish, a heterogeneous mass truly representative both of the human flotsam and the sturdy American manhood which comprise the civil population of New York City."[3]

Yet, this incredible diversity was not limited to the 77th Division. Other US Army units would find themselves dealing with the complexity of integrating vast numbers of foreign-born men into their ranks. During the First World War, the ranks of the American Expeditionary Forces (AEF) were filled with men—some willing to obey orders and others not—who could understand only a very few words of the commands they were given. A good number of them were unable to read or write in their own native languages yet now were expected to perform dangerous tasks in obedience to orders given in English.

It is estimated that some 20 percent of the soldiers in the US Army were foreign born. With the size of the army in France—or still training in the States at the time of the 11 November 1918 Armistice—being almost four million strong, this would indicate a foreign-born contingent of almost 800,000 men. Where did they come from? And what brought them here? In answering these questions, this book will provide an inside look at an amazing story of how the US military overcame the challenge of training and deploying these many men and women, and in doing so opened the doors of citizenship to thousands of worthy soldiers.

A key feature of Hollywood filmmaking has always been the ability to make the implausible appear real. Even in 1917, US film studios tried to give a heroic aura to the hell that was taking place on the Western Front. Here, soldiers from four Allied armies—Italy, Great Britain, France, and the United States (for some reason Belgium was excluded from the picture)—charge forward together. *Courtesy Library of Congress*

It is important to also consider the plight of the tens of thousands of native-born and foreign-born men drafted in late spring and summer 1918. Most of them were sent to National Army divisions preparing to go overseas; they deployed with minimal training, and many ended up becoming replacements for combat divisions that had already suffered heavily in the fighting in France. It was common to find men assigned as replacements who just five or six weeks earlier had been civilians. These men had to quickly assimilate into a combat unit and blend into an existing cohesive force. This is not an easy task for anyone; compound this difficulty with a language barrier, and one can begin to understand the feelings of the foreign-born soldier thrust into such a position.

It must be said that not all foreign-born members of the US military worked under the handicap of not understanding English; there were many soldiers of Irish, Scottish, Welsh, Australian, English, or Canadian birth who served in the US Army. There were also a great number of men who had immigrated to the United States long enough before the war to know English, find employment, raise a family, and in some cases serve in the Regular Army, or in a local National Guard unit. The vast majority who entered the US military through the simple process of being found eligible for service by a local draft board were recent arrivals.

Another aspect of the challenge was that not all foreign countries were treated the same. Foreign-born men, usually referred to in the period of study as "aliens," were considered to belong in one of three categories: "Co-belligerent," meaning they were from France, Belgium, Russia, Japan, Italy, Great Britain, or its Commonwealth; "Belligerent," meaning they were from Germany, Turkey, or a country that was part of the Austro-Hungarian or Ottoman Empire; or they were "Neutral," which implied origins from one of the Scandinavian countries, the Netherlands, Mexico, Ireland, or

Poster makers and Liberty Bond–selling organizations used the same approach as Hollywood. In this example, a stylized view of a handsome American soldier and his beloved mother encourage the viewer to support the war effort by buying bonds. *Courtesy Library of Congress*

This is a more realistic picture of the American soldier and family of 1917: a Virginia Doughboy poses with his sister and parents before leaving for France. Note that his mother, instead of demanding the viewer support the war, appears unable to look directly at the camera. People growing up in Virginia's Shenandoah Valley after the Civil War knew full well the price that war exacts on soldiers and on farmland; her face reflects that knowledge.

other countries not aligned with the countries at war. These distinctions will carry great weight and have very serious implications when this story progresses.

Underlying all these categories was a further differentiation: "declarant" men. These were men who had legally declared their intention to become a US citizen. Nondeclarant, cobelligerent aliens were exempt from the US draft and were entitled to request exemption at the time of registration. By requesting an exemption, a man was not only exempting himself from the draft, but also making himself a potential target for expulsion from the country or harassment and scrutiny by local "patriotic" organizations. It might also make him eligible to be conscripted into the military of his native country. It was a tough choice, and not one made lightly. Most of the men in this category, either through ignorance or willingness to serve, waived their right to claim exemption.

Despite the many different problems with aliens and the associated headaches they caused unit commanders, for the most part the men turned out to be good soldiers. Even as iconic an All-American Doughboy as Sgt. Alvin York would later attest to their combative spirit and willingness to take on the foe.[4]

The presence of aliens in the ranks also provided a bit of rough humor for the soldiers. In an oft-repeated joke, the Camp Travis history reported that:

Poles and Bohemians were numerous among the recruits, and such names as Czsertozc Mjovscek were frequent. As a result, when the first sergeant of one company sneezed while taking roll call, fourteen of his men answered, "Here."[5]

Other ethnic and race relations aspects of the period were not quite so humorous. A soldier from the 168th Infantry Regiment—an Iowa National Guard unit—recounted how he helped run off the "Jew" merchant who was selling candy and snacks to the Doughboys.[6] It got worse. A German-born Lutheran minister in upstate New York was prohibited from delivering Sunday services to his congregation in German—the common

For the immigrant family, there is little of the heroic aspect in this portrait. For many foreign-born men such as soldier Vincent Presta, service in the US military has often been a rite of passage on the road to citizenship. That rite does not make it any easier for the soldier or his mother. *Courtesy Rose Presta Pennington*

language of the assembly—even though his son was in France serving in the AEF. Worse yet was the case of Robert Praeger in Indiana. Rejected for military service for having only one eye, Praeger made the mistake of being overheard criticizing President Wilson. Arrested and jailed, German-born Praeger was taken from the jail by a mob and was lynched. After a short trial, all eleven of his killers were found "not guilty."[7]

This is not an exhaustive treatment of the topic, and not all nationalities are represented (although we certainly have included *almost* all of them in this book). It is based largely on research in unpublished sources, private collections, family histories, and public archives.

Archives accessible through Ancestry.com® are rich and mostly untapped for purposes such as ours, but they naturally tend to steer the data in the direction of whatever sources have been digitized. Readers will notice some states more heavily represented than others, and this is due to the accessibility of unpublished, primary source materials. This is a limitation but not a liability. The consulted sources are important, and this volume will bring to light the accomplishments of a great number of men who have thus far gone unmentioned in World War I historiography.

In 1919, Congress passed a law requiring the War Department to compile a record of each veteran's wartime service and supply it to each veteran's home state in the form of a statement-of-service card. Each man's service record was used to obtain the information for the cards, including name, date, and place of birth; serial number; ranks held; units and dates of assignment; dates of overseas service; battles; and wounds. Although the data on the cards is sometimes incomplete, and the cards are not always easily accessible, they are a treasure trove for researchers and historians. Cards for some states are readily available online, and we have relied on these for examples to show overall trends. Likewise, we have found various online archives, many through Ancestry.com®, with various records that shed light on the experience of American soldiers during the war.

Perhaps the most important point the authors can make is that through following this little-traveled path of history, we have developed an incredible respect for the foreign-born soldiers of the period.

As authors, we at first struggled with how to organize and present the material. Should we segregate the information by country of birth, or by unit of assignment? Neither approach proved viable, so ultimately we decided to start the story from the beginning with the draft and follow the evolution of the soldiers as they passed through their training phase, naturalization process, deployment to France, combat operations, and finally either their return home or continued service in the Army of Occupation. In following this

approach, we ended with a product much like the US military of the period: on any given page you may have an Italian-born soldier's photo next to an Irishman and a Greek. A Scot's picture may appear next to a photograph of Dutchmen. So be it.

We also made a conscious decision to let these Doughboys tell the story in their own words. We have chosen to use their words as they wrote them and intentionally avoided the use of "[sic]" to correct their spelling, capitalization, or punctuation. Where we felt it necessary or helpful, we did add words in brackets to assist the reader in shaping the story. In some cases we had to translate or find translators to help us understand something the soldiers wrote in their native language.

The war and the Spanish flu changed America while the soldiers were away in France or in training camps. People on the home front had also sacrificed for the cause, and not everyone wanted to hear about a Doughboy's adventures.

For many, the 1920s would roar and then crash. Some foreign-born soldiers would find that the camaraderie of the trenches had reverted back to the same anti-

A cartoon by Capt. Alban B. Butler Jr., 1st Division, called on humorous images to show the various ethnic groups and nationalities represented in this famous division. *Courtesy 1st Division Museum at Cantigny*

foreigner attitudes they had faced before the war. Yet many also found that their service and newly minted citizenship had bought them a place in American society, and they thrived.

Just as in the Meuse-Argonne, each would experience the same event differently. As authors, we have tried to show as many origins and facets of the foreign-born soldiers as we could to give the reader this incredible story. If it appears at times that Italian-born soldiers are overrepresented in this work, there is a good reason: Italian-born men made up an incredibly high percentage of the foreign-born men in the military. The *World War Service Record for Rochester and Monroe County: Those Who Died for Us* lists the names of the 609 men and women from the city of Rochester, New York, and surrounding areas who died of all causes in the war. Of those 609, forty-one were Italian-born men who died in combat, another thirteen died from the flu, and two died from accidents in training, for a total of fifty-six. Therefore, more than 12 percent of Rochester's war dead were born in Italy. Of the remaining 553, there were also a surprising number of Canadians, Germans, Austrians, and British, but none in numbers close to the Italians.

Ultimately, this is not as much a story about numbers and statistics as it is about Doughboys. As US military veterans, we were very proud to be given the opportunity to write this book, but this is their story to tell much more than it is ours. We ask that you look at their pictures, read their words, and respect their struggles and accomplishments. An army at war is an incredibly stressful organization, with little tolerance for errors or misunderstandings. Imagine being in that environment and understanding only every third or fourth word.

For many years it has been popular to disparage the contributions of the AEF in ending the war, particularly among those who claim that Germany was on her last legs when the Doughboys arrived. Taking nothing away from the heroic efforts of the British, French, Belgian, and Italian armies, the German army of late 1917 and 1918 still

Some foreign-born Doughboys found much to like in the US military and decided to remain in uniform after the war. Among them was Italian-born Charley Pastori. He chose to remain with the US Army of Occupation in the German Rhineland rather than return to his prewar home in St. Louis.

had a lot of fight left in it. Army Chief of Staff Gen. Peyton March pointed out in his 1932 book *The Nation at War* that the Allies had already conceded 1918 as a year for defense while awaiting the arrival of the American force in numbers great enough to defeat the enemy in 1919.[8] Consequently, the AEF's massive effort in the Meuse-Argonne, and in support of the British Army, truly proved to be the tipping force that brought the Germans to the armistice rail car. Numbered among the Doughboys of the American army were so many foreign-born soldiers that it is impossible not to see their fingerprints on the Springfields and Enfields that broke the Hindenburg Line. This, then, is our attempt to tell their story and to show you their faces. Lest we forget.

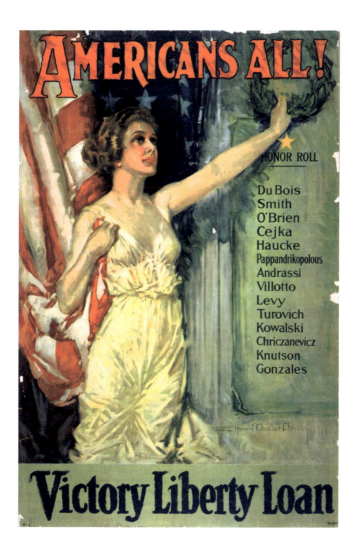

## CHAPTER ONE

# A NATION OF
# IMMIGRANTS

And what of the poor bewildered alien himself? . . . [O]ught we not commend those great millions for their steadiness of purpose and action, their loyalty and decency under trying conditions? Our debt to them rests with the future and American patriots for payment.[1]

America is a nation of immigrants, and it is no surprise that many of them have served in her military. Especially during the Civil War, many immigrants flocked to the colors while still others were drafted. Most of these men were from old-stock immigrant groups. There were entire regiments composed of German or Irish immigrants. Almost all European nations, and several non-European nations, were represented. One of the most colorful of the Union regiments, the 39th New York Infantry, Garibaldi Guard, consisted of five companies of Germans and one company each of French, Hungarians, Italians, Spanish, and Swiss.[2]

According to historian James McPherson, about 25 percent of the white soldiers who served in the Union Army were foreign born. Reflecting the nature of prewar immigration, most of these men were German, Irish, or British. Approximately 216,000 were born in Germany, 50,000 were born in England, and 20,000 were French Canadians from Quebec. There were also thousands of Scandinavian (Norwegian, Swedish, Finnish, and Danish), Dutch, Polish, Italian, Swiss, and Mexican soldiers. And there was a sprinkling of men from other countries, such as China, Portugal, and Spain, among others.[3]

It is difficult to determine the precise numbers of different nationalities of men serving in the Union Army during the Civil War. Due to the changing nature of nations and empires, Germans, Poles, Russians, and Hungarians all could be classified in different ways. Likewise, generally the numbers change if one counts militia, state guards, etc.

Agreeing with McPherson's figure, historian Ella Lonn estimated that 518,161 foreign-born men served in the Union Army during the war—between 20 and 25 percent of the total forces. Among those, according to Lonn, were over 200,000 Germans, 144,221 Irish, 53,532 Canadians, 54,508 English, 3,000 Swedes, 4,200 Norwegians, 4,000 Poles, and 800 Hungarians, in addition to thousands from other countries.[4] Lonn's and McPherson's estimates, which exclude African American soldiers from their computations, are probably much closer to the actual totals than Bell I. Wiley's estimate, who asserted that in the Union Army, "about one out of every twenty or twenty-five was of alien birth . . ."[5]

The wave of immigration that began around 1880 differed from earlier waves in several important characteristics. These immigrants primarily came from southern and eastern Europe, whereas the earlier waves tended to come from northwestern Europe and the British Isles. Second, the goal of many of the new immigrants was to secure employment in growing American industries, with some planning to return to Europe later, rather than to resettle their families in the New World. Third, and related to the second, many of the new immigrants were young men without family members accompanying them.

The volume and duration of immigration after 1880 guaranteed that there would be large numbers of foreign-born, military-age men available in America's manpower pool. Between 1891 and 1910, approximately 12.5 million immigrants came to the United States, most of them from countries in southern and eastern Europe.[6]

Italians were among the most numerous of the post-1880 wave of immigrants. From 1891 to 1914, approximately 3,587,066 Italians came to the United States.[7] Most of these were single men looking for work in the rapidly industrializing United States. They found work in factories in urban areas of the East and Midwest, or on the railroads snaking their way across the West and the northwestern prairies.

The Italians, more than any other immigrant group, were likely to return to their homeland. The early immigrants in the 1880s and 1890s tended to be poor farmers or landless laborers who sought work to obtain money; they then planned to return to Italy, buy a little land, and start a family. Although some followed this plan exactly, many more became "birds of passage," making seasonal trips between Italy and the United States and generating money during each sojourn in the States. Soon these men brought wives and children to America.

Immigrants from Austria-Hungary and Russia included, among others, Croatians, Slovaks, Czechs, Ruthenians [Ukrainians], Poles, Lithuanians, Latvians, Slovenes, and Jews of various nationalities. Poor economic and agricultural conditions drove many of these migrants to seek work and land in the United States.[8] Similar migrant groups included the Turks, Armenians, and Greeks.

Spain and Portugal also sent their sons and daughters to the Americas, but most went to the Spanish- and Portuguese-speaking countries of Central and South America. Surprisingly, the United States was the second most popular choice for Portuguese immigrants behind Brazil. The largest annual number (some 14,171) came in 1913, and most of them were fishermen from the Azores. They mainly settled in New England or California.[9]

Immigrants from the earliest waves continued to come to the United States after 1880. Between 1891 and 1914, approximately 910,000 Germans immigrated to the

United States.[10] German return migration was comparatively small; by the 1880s, they, as a people, had a firm foundation in the States, helping to minimize repatriation.

Although immigrants from the British Isles were part of the older wave, others also came during the new wave. Between 1891 and 1914, approximately 2,795,000 immigrated to the United States, broken down as follows: 1,451,000 from England and Wales, 973,000 from Ireland, and 370,000 from Scotland.[11] Although in the 1880s many British immigrants were single men looking for work and a return to Britain with a bit more money, others, especially those coming after 1890, sought land, work, and a permanent home in the United States.[12]

Scandinavians continued to come to the States throughout this period. Swedes and Norwegians had been coming in force since the 1840s; Danes were next, beginning in the 1870s; and Finns followed starting in the 1880s. Many Scandinavians settled in the Midwest, where they started farms and homesteads on the Great Plains.[13]

Asian immigrants of this time consisted mostly of Chinese and Japanese laborers. Chinese men were recruited for work on the Central Pacific Railroad in the mid- to late 1860s, during construction of the Transcontinental Railroad. Others followed, and by the 1880s, "Chinese constituted about half of the farm laborers in California."[14] Anti-Chinese sentiments, particularly in California, soon led Congress to pass the 1882 Exclusion Act, suspending Chinese immigration for ten years. Many Japanese then came to California to fill the need for farm labor. From 1898—when Hawaii was annexed by the United States—until 1903, about 60,000 Japanese entered the United States.[15]

The US/Mexico border has always been porous, and official immigration statistics show over 700,000 Mexicans entering the States between 1901 and 1930; the actual number of arrivals was almost certainly higher. Here, too, figures can be distorted because of the large number of transient and seasonal workers.[16]

Thus, America's involvement in the Spanish American War in 1898 occurred in the middle of this mass migration from southern and eastern Europe. An examination of Pennsylvania's Veteran's Compensation Applications for service during the Spanish American War, China Relief Expedition, or the Philippine Insurrection from 1898 to 1902 yields some interesting rough figures. Considering only men born in countries supplying the majority of immigrants in the new wave, we find the following countries represented: Russia, 71; Poland, 36; Hungary, 34; Italy, 22; Czechoslovakia, 5; Romania, 2; Armenia, 1; and Greece, 1.[17]

The majority of the soldiers in World War I were born between 1886 and 1900, so we can assume most foreign-born soldiers came to the United States between 1890 and 1914. There are exceptions, of course: Joseph Barchi, who served in the US Navy, was born in Italy in 1879 and came with his family in 1880; and at the other extreme, Jan Soer, who served in the 9th Trench Mortar Battery, was born in the Netherlands in 1890 and came to the United States on 5 March 1916.[18] Examining immigration statistics for these years provides a rough idea of how many of a given immigrant nationality group were present in the country on the eve of the war. It should be remembered that there are always difficulties determining numbers because of differing methods of counting and classifying passengers; plus, many people who came to the

States later returned to their country of birth and are not counted in records showing numbers of actual residents in the United States.

The foreign-born elements of the top-five immigrant groups in the United States in 1910 were 2,311,000 Germans, 1,352,000 Irish, 1,343,000 Italians, 1,184,000 Russians, and 938,000 Poles. Due to the nature of immigration from many of these countries, a large percentage of these immigrants were draft-age men. This is especially true of the later emigrations from southern and eastern Europe: Italy, Greece, Hungary (including those nations in the Austro-Hungarian Empire), Poland, and Russia.[19]

For better or worse for the individuals involved, the recent arrival of so many draft-age men would certainly prove of immense value to the United States. The issue now facing the government was the matter of whom to draft, and equally important, how to deal with the large numbers of men who came from "enemy" countries.

## CHAPTER TWO

# DRAFT LAWS, DRAFT REGISTRATION, AND DRAFTED MEN

In 1863, a Provost Marshal General's Bureau was . . . [charged] with raising the necessary armed forces for the conduct of the war, either by voluntary enlistment or draft. However . . . only 46,347 men out of 776,829 conscripts actually joined the colors during the Civil War. Moreover, the enforcement of the draft provoked riot and protest throughout the Nation and reduced the city of New York to a state of anarchy.[1]

Even before the United States entered World War I on 6 April 1917, most military, and many civilian officials, knew the US Army was not ready to fight the kind of war being waged in Europe. The Regular Army stood at about 128,000 men, while the National Guard mustered about 67,000 men still in federal service, mostly returning from the Mexican border or guarding key industrial sites, bridges, or ammunition plants.[2] Clearly more men would be needed. In addition to infantry, artillery, and engineer troops, the army required a bewildering variety of other units.

Men were needed for all types of supply, administration, ordnance, transportation, and medical duties. Special units performed railroad construction and operation, forestry, water supply and treatment, butchery, bakery, laundry, and other duties. Patriotic fervor alone was not enough to build an army capable of making a difference in the war; the United States would have to resort to a national draft.

Additionally, President Wilson believed that a nationally conscripted army would be more representative of American ideals. This belief supported his statement that America's entry in the war was not for national gain, but to establish a peaceful world. There was strong opposition by several southern congressmen to the concept of universal drafting of men for the US military. While they publicly claimed that

**Official Government Notice**

# EVERY MAN

Between the ages of 18 to 45 (both inclusive), except those previously registered

# MUST REGISTER

for the

## *Selective Service Draft*

Exact date of registration to be announced by Official Proclamation. Be ready, find out when to register, and where to register. Registration will take place early in

# SEPTEMBER

*Penalty for Failure to Register*

is one year imprisonment, and NO man can exonerate himself by the payment of a fine.

# Register Promptly!

E. H. CROWDER
Provost Marshal General
War Department, U. S. A.

(Read Other Side Carefully)

The first draft registration included all men aged twenty-one to thirty-one but did not generate enough manpower for the Army. Accordingly, there needed to be a second draft. Shown here is the official notice from the government announcing the second draft's new, expanded age limits and setting early September 1918 as the date by which registration was required. *Courtesy National Archives*

conscription would lead to a rise of militarism in the country and that it was un-American to force men into the Army, their true motives were obvious to many people. These congressmen disapproved of the draft because they feared it would provide military training to the African Americans in their states, perhaps giving them the means to force racial equality.

Assistant Army Chief of Staff Maj. Gen. Tasker H. Bliss saw through the subterfuge and wrote that the southerners did not like "the idea of looking forward five or six years by which time their entire male negro population will have been trained to arms."[3] Despite the objections of the southerners and other antiwar congressmen, President Wilson and Secretary of War Newton Baker persevered and were able to move conscription legislation through Congress; the Selective Service Act, as passed, ensured it would be organized under strictly civilian oversight.

The Selective Service Act of 1917 was designed to fix many of the problems that bedeviled the North during the Civil War, when a similar conscription act was established. The Act of 1917 authorized a selective draft of all eligible males between ages twenty-one and thirty-one and specifically prohibited a selectee from buying his way out of service by replacing himself with a "substitute."* The administration of the registration process and subsequent draft was entrusted to local draft boards composed of civic leaders in each community or town. However, the overall administration of the draft required a large national-level organization with branches focused on specific areas of the process, including:

STATE OF NEW YORK
MILITARY CENSUS OF NEW YORK CITY
# NOTICE
1. Be sure you understand each question before answering it.
2. You are required by law to SIGN YOUR NAME on the registration form and on the certificate of registration.
3. You are entitled to a CERTIFICATE of REGISTRATION. Do not leave without it.
4. If you are a male CITIZEN between 18 and 45 be sure you receive a NOTICE ABOUT EXEMPTION and a CERTIFICATE of REGISTRATION.
5. Have you a relative or friend who does not understand English? If so bring him with you and help him register.
6. Have you a sick or disabled relative who must register? If so report it to the Census Agent.
7. When you have registered please
DO NOT LOITER ABOUT THE BUILDING
E. P. GOODRICH
Director Military Census, New York City

One of the New York State announcements for military census of New York City. It clearly reminds citizens that if they have friends or relatives who do not speak English, they should help them register for the draft.

Publication Division: responsible for producing the required forms and documents and ensuring their timely delivery to each board.

Administrative Division: responsible for resolving questions from local and district boards and the specialized legal and medical boards.

Registration Division: responsible for the actual operation of the draft process and issuing draft and registration numbers. It was also responsible for "status" determinations and resolving issues involving critical occupations that could exempt registrants from military service.

Appeals Division: provide recommendations on draft appeals sent to the president.

Statistics Division: responsible for determining and reporting occupations of selected men to ensure that career fields deemed critical, such as the defense industry, were not stripped of all their workers.

Classification Division: resolve questions of classification of registrants, as well as determining excusable delays or absences from reporting.

Information Division: serve as the central clearing house for information about the draft.

Inspection and Investigation Division: responsible for investigating complaints against specific boards or board members.

Law Division: resolve legal questions concerning the selective-service process and questions of procedures. This division did not handle questions involving citizenship, international law, or alien status issues.

---

* During the Civil War, the use of substitutes had been one of the most despised features of the conscription act, because it allowed those citizens with sufficient money to pay their way out of serving by providing someone in their place.

Universal conscription meant that men in all the states and territories were subject to the draft. This poster was produced during the first draft of men aged twenty-one to thirty-one and was a reminder of that fact. It was used in the Hawaiian Islands to ensure everyone knew their responsibilities and would register on time. *Courtesy Library of Congress*

Medical Division: responsible for all aspects of medical rules and regulations concerning physical requirements and medical examinations.

Aliens Division: perhaps most important for our purpose; was responsible for handling all questions related to classification and deferment of aliens. The Aliens Division was also authorized to resolve all questions involving citizenship, international law, and passports.[4]

Assisting the local draft boards were a number of other civic organizations, including the American Medical Association, assisting in the selection of members for medical boards; the National Dental Association and the Preparedness League of American Dentists, which offered free examinations to draftees and military personnel; the American Red Cross, which provided personnel at railway stations to assist selected men while traveling to training camps; and the American Bar Association, which provided legal services.[5]

The terms of the 1917 Act allowed for a number of exemptions from conscription: family dependency, employment in an occupation essential to the war effort, and certain alien statuses or personal religious beliefs. Regardless, registering was required for all male citizens in the designated age group. Only after registration would any of the draft exemptions be considered, and then on a case-by-case basis.

The country was divided into draft districts, using a population of approximately 30,000 as the guideline for establishment of a local board. Each district board was responsible for approximately 2,100 men. There were 4,648 local draft boards nationwide (including the territories), with 14,416 board members, 155 district boards, and 1,319 medical boards.[6] For example, the city of Philadelphia had fifty-one draft boards, while the smaller city of Baltimore had twenty-four.[7]

These boards registered the men, performed initial screening and classification, and issued draft cards that included the draft number given to each prospective draftee when he reported. The numbers were later drawn in a national lottery, and all men holding that particular number at each draft board

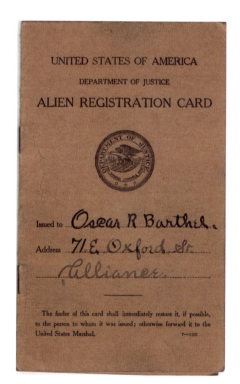

UNITED STATES OF AMERICA

DEPARTMENT OF JUSTICE

ALIEN REGISTRATION CARD

Issued to *Oscar R Barthel*

Address *71 E. Oxford St.*

*Alliance*

The finder of this card shall immediately restore it, if possible, to the person to whom it was issued; otherwise forward it to the United States Marshal.

The alien registration card issued by the US Department of Justice to Oscar R. Barthel, a German-born man living in Alliance, Ohio. After registering as an "enemy alien," Barthel was required to have this card with him at all times or risk being jailed.

were considered drafted. On 5 June 1917, almost ten million men registered for the draft. Surprisingly, this number was to prove inadequate, since a very large number of men were either exempted by deferment or found to be mentally or physically unfit to be soldiers. The classes of draft eligibility were:

**I. Eligible and liable for military service:** unmarried men and married men either with independent spouses or a child over age sixteen.
**II. Temporarily deferred but available for military service:** married men with dependent spouses and children under age sixteen.
**III. Temporarily exempted but available for military service:** local officials, men who were sole sources of income for dependent parents, or men employed in farming or industry essential to the war effort.
**IV. Exempted due to extreme hardship:** men who were the sole source of income for their spouses, children, or other family members, such as dependent brothers or sisters.
**V. Exempted or ineligible:** state or federal officials, men already serving in the US military, pilots, members of the clergy and divinity school students, men who were physically or mentally disabled, criminals, enemy aliens, and resident aliens.

By far the largest deferment category was IV, which was based on the registrant's "family dependency." The next-largest grouping of deferments was category V: a consolidation of those deferred for alien status, already being in the military, or suffering from disability. The size of the exemption for reason of physical disability group was quite large and is almost counterintuitive, since we usually think of the people of this period as living healthier, robust lives. In fact, as the National Guard discovered while mobilizing for the Mexican border campaign in 1916, a very large number of eligible men were physically unacceptable for military service. The causes included malnourishment, missing appendages, deafness, deformities such as "club foot," and obesity.

Ultimately, of the first ten million registrants, over half a million received a physical deferment. Another problem was that many of the men already serving on active duty in the US Army or Navy never bothered to inform their local draft board and were therefore carried on the draft board "books" as deserters. This proved particularly embarrassing in 1921, when the draft board in Passaic, New Jersey, released a "slacker list" of men who they believed had avoided the draft by not registering. The list included Joseph Brottovich, a Doughboy from the 29th Division who had been gassed twice and wounded three times in the Argonne.[8]

The US War Department recognized that the war in Europe was consuming vast quantities of manpower, and it was projected the United States would require a massive army. Therefore, the age range for draft registration was expanded to include all males from eighteen to forty-five years old. Two additional registrations were decreed: 5 June and 24 August 1918 (both considered the second registration period) and 12 September 1918. By the end of the war, under the new guidelines the total number of men registered had increased to 23,908,576.

Of this total, there were reportedly 489,003 who refused to appear before their board and were therefore considered "deserters." The number of "deserters" was reduced to 337,649 when men who were determined to already be serving in the military were subtracted. Of this number, 163,738 were apprehended by the authorities and punished. Interestingly, while registration and drafting was suspended after the 11 November Armistice, the search for and punishment of draft evaders continued much longer.[9]

President Woodrow Wilson's decision to rely primarily on conscription rather than voluntary enlistment alone to raise the manpower needed for the army meant that considerable thought had to be given to the issue of recent immigrants and resident aliens as part of the manpower pool. The Selective Service Act of 1917 included "declarant aliens" as potential draftees. A resident alien became "declarant" by having filed for US citizenship, and he was therefore eligible for the draft.

On the other hand, three groups of aliens were excluded by the 1917 act: those in the diplomatic services of foreign countries, those who had not declared themselves as desiring to become an American citizen, and those considered to be from an "enemy" country. This last group included all those who originated from Germany, the various countries of the Austro-Hungarian Empire, Bulgaria, and Turkey. When the United States entered the war there were an estimated 500,000 German and three million Austro-Hungarian citizens residing in the United States. While these numbers included many women, children, and elderly men, there still remained a large number of draft-age men in these groups.

During 5 June 1917 to 12 September 1918, a total of 1,703,006 aliens registered for the draft. Later research concluded that at least forty-six different languages were spoken by these men. Somewhat surprisingly, given the United States' very recent occupation of Vera Cruz and the Punitive Expedition into Mexico, there were even 5,700 Mexican men who had either volunteered or been drafted into the US military.[10]

Interestingly, a very large number of "enemy aliens" in the third excluded category chose to refuse the exclusion while registering for the draft, thereby demonstrating their willingness to join the US armed forces if selected. What was not surprising was the rush for permits when the US government announced that any enemy aliens needed permission to work or live within a half mile of a "Federal or State arsenal or armory or other military establishment."[11] In the large Atlantic seaboard port cities such as Philadelphia, New York, and Boston, it was difficult not to live within a half mile of some key military or government facility involved in the war effort. Many aliens needed these permits just to be able to continue to work at their current jobs or remain in their homes.

The registration and induction of aliens—declarants and nondeclarants—were fraught with legal and diplomatic issues. The War Department initially exempted nondeclarant aliens from the draft if they claimed such an exemption at the time of registration. In fact, "the regulations and instructions required local and district boards to give every alien, as well as every other registrant, a full and fair hearing, or a full and fair opportunity to be heard, on any claim of exemption that he might have."[12] However, "the mass of foreign-born residents were themselves permeated by the

A rare document: the work permit for German-born Christian Grube, allowing him to live and work in the Bronx and then later in Hoboken. Note that he is allowed to pass through "forbidden areas" in the course of his work but was not allowed to be within 100 yards of any waterfront. Grube was twenty-eight at the time of the first draft in 1917 and was required to register even though he was technically an "enemy alien."

The registration card for Patrick Healey, an Irishman from West Sligo, listing his occupation as a laborer. As with many names of the period, on his official records it alternates between Haley and Healey. His signature is not helpful, since he made his mark instead of writing his name. Healey would go on to serve in the 80th Division in France. *Courtesy the Rhodes and Smergalski families*

spirit of readiness to waive their exemptions and voluntarily accept the call to military service. Thousands of nondeclarant aliens of cobelligerent and even of neutral origin welcomed the opportunity to take up arms against the arch enemy of all . . ." Local draft boards reported that 191,491 of these nondeclarant aliens refused to claim exemption and were therefore eligible for the draft.[13]

Certainly many of these men may not have understood their rights, and some must have been inducted against their will. As the provost marshal general's report stated: "Without a doubt there were rare and sporadic local instances of carelessness and of bias which led to improper inductions. The zeal of some local boards, irritated by the slacker spirit of some classes of population, resulted occasionally in such improprieties."[14]

This led to some men being sent to training camps, only to be discharged shortly thereafter for physical, mental, or country-of-origin reasons. Not all men who were discharged as enemy aliens were hostile to the United States; some indeed desired to serve in the US Army. Essa Albert was born in "Palestine, Turkey" in 1892 and entered service from Pittsburgh, Pennsylvania, on 27 May 1918. Albert was assigned to "Co. A, 45th Engrs., Hdq. Detachment, Reclamation Division" until 28 August 1918, when he was discharged as an enemy alien. In 1934, Albert filed for a Pennsylvania state veteran's bonus. To the application form's question, "Did you ever

Each man who was not immediately exempted after registering for the draft later received a letter informing him of the time and place to appear for a more complete physical examination. Here is the letter from the Fresno Draft Board sent to Haroatun "Harry" Sarkisian, an Armenian man born in Harpoot, Turkey. Sarkisian had graduated from the University of Southern California and was a self-employed lawyer when he received his notice to appear.

refuse on conscientious, political or other grounds to perform full military duty or to render unqualified service," Albert answered, "No—I was discharged for alienage, but not at my own request." Albert had to wait until 19 February 1937 to find out that his claim was disapproved.[15]

For the allied/cobelligerent countries, the US government agreed to "reciprocal treaties of conscription."[16] These treaties "provided that alien residents should be allowed an opportunity to enlist in the forces of their own governments, and that, failing to do so within a prescribed time, they should become subject to the selective draft regulations of the country in which they were residing."[17]

For all three draft registration periods, a total of 3,877,083 aliens registered; of these, 1,270,182 were declarants and 2,606,901 were nondeclarants. Further, of these, 2,228,980 were from cobelligerent countries (57.5% of the total alien registration), 636,601 were from neutral countries (16.4% of the total alien registration), and 1,011,502 were from enemy and allied enemy countries (26.1% of the total alien registration). During the period of the initial draft, almost half a million immigrants from all countries were registered.

The addition of these men to the manpower pool was quite welcome, but there remained concerns about adding them to the fighting force, such as their loyalty, and their ability to understand and obey orders in a language different from their own. Ultimately, these concerns forced the US Army to develop training procedures that accommodated ethnic differences and language barriers. Officers and noncommissioned officers (NCOs) were required to take into consideration not only the ethnic background of their soldiers, but also any dietary constraints imposed by religious differences.

The draft registration, conducted at a local board and administered by local residents, provided the first opportunity for a cursory physical review of the registrant. The board's clerk recorded the answer for each registrant to the question: "Has person lost arm, leg, hand, foot, or both eyes, or is he otherwise disabled (specify)?" Also, the registrant was given the opportunity to claim exemption from the draft (for any of the reasons stated above) at this time.

After registration, any man selected by the board for service would later be notified to report for an examination to determine his fitness to serve in the US military. Once there, the prospective draftee would answer some general questions about his health, and a doctor would give him a physical examination that covered his weight, height, and other physical measurements, as well as a hearing and a vision test. The exam also covered the man's nose, throat, heart, lungs, feet, genito-urinary organs, and teeth, as well as checking for hernia or hemorrhoids. Finally, the doctor would indicate to which physical category group the man should be assigned. The physical categories were:

**Group A:** Vigorous men without any defects that would prevent them from full military duty.
**Group B:** Men with diseases, physical defects, or abnormalities that could be cured.
**Group C:** Men below standard for full duty but capable of performing some service.
**Group D:** Men physically unfit for military service.

Later, after the registrant had returned to his home, the local draft board would ratify the doctor's findings. The combination of draft eligibility category (seen earlier) with the physical categories created a Roman numeral/alphabetic rating, such as IA, IIA, IVB, or VE. This combination gave a clear picture of the individual's status and his likelihood of being chosen in the draft. After the combination was determined, each man was notified of his status and given a five-day period to appeal his classification.

Another important point to be made is that "universal conscription" truly meant that all men in the designated age groups must register for the draft. While nowhere near the numbers of men from Italy, Ireland, and Poland, there were men born in African countries such as Dahomey, Liberia, and Portuguese West Africa (Angola) living in the United States, and they too were subject to the draft. *Courtesy Chuck Thomas Collection*

For those found both eligible and physically fit—primarily those determined to be IA or IB—their selection was a forgone conclusion. Sometime thereafter they would receive a card notifying them to get their affairs in order and to be ready to be called at any time. It is significant to note that the manpower needs of the Army were so great in 1918 that prewar standards and the subsequent physical requirements established in 1917 were greatly reduced when the second draft was conducted.[18]

When the fighting ended on 11 November 1918, the selective service had provided 2,758,542 men to the military (while about two million more voluntarily enlisted) and was examining some 7,500,000 more for potential service. The provost marshal estimated that on the basis of previous statistics, this would have provided another 3,630,542 men for military service.[19]

Of the almost three million men who were eventually drafted into the US Army, almost 400,000 of them were African Americans, with the remainder being white, Hispanic, Asian, or Native American. As is the nature of all large organizations and bureaucracies, there were complaints that draft boards were not completely impartial. Critics argued that some boards were rendering their decisions on exempting registrants more on the basis of their social class or community standing than the validity of their individual situation. In particular, farmers were more likely to be drafted than industrial workers solely on the basis of the "critical war effort" exemption that valued factory work over farm labor.

With the registration process completed for each individual, eligibility determined, and draft sequence numbers drawn, the men who were not exempted were considered "selected" for military service. It is interesting to note that officials of the period used the word "selectee" or "selected" in place of draftee. It was believed by officials that "selected" implied a measure of exclusivity and honor.

What the "selected" men believed about the honor of being selected is a matter of debate. They were informed that they would soon receive instructions on where and when to report for their training. Once called for service, the men assembled at their local draft board for transportation to the nearest military camp for induction and processing, and to begin their training and military service.

Now that the US Army had to prepare for combat against a well-disciplined, technically proficient, and highly professional German army, the selected men would receive the best training the country could manage to provide. It would require that native-born and foreign-born soldiers alike receive focused training under tough conditions before these fledgling American troops would be ready for combat. The first step would be the reception process at one of the many training camps quickly being constructed across the country.

## CHAPTER THREE

# STATESIDE TRAINING AND SERVICE

The huge cantonments . . . were really cities, but cities of a type and built for a purpose . . . The long wooden barracks, mess halls, hospitals, and office buildings covered hundreds of acres of land and possessed all the attributes of a modern city except for the quality of permanence.[1]

At first, there was a significant difference between the soldiers going to the National Army training camps and those going to National Guard training camps. Foreign-born soldiers in the National Guard—and there were many—either were recent volunteers or had been serving in Guard units before the outbreak of war. Likewise, there were already a large number of foreign-born soldiers in the Regular Army and Marine Corps.

Therefore, the Regular Army, Marines, and National Guard were basically a volunteer force. On the other end of the spectrum, the selected men—native born and foreign born alike—from the first draft were sent to National Army training sites. This meant these men would be trained primarily in the North; of the sixteen large National Army camps, only four were located in the South, while nearly all of the sixteen National Guard camps were in the South. There was also a significant difference between the two types of camps: the National Army camps would have wooden buildings for barracks, while the Guard units would have tents. By September 1917, the training camps were already under construction, and trainloads of selected men were traveling to their training sites while the Guard and Regular Army units were heading for theirs.

When the decision was made to establish the thirty-two divisional training sites throughout the country, the War Department took a number of factors into consideration. First and foremost was that some camp space was also going to be required to assemble and train the regiments of Regular Army divisions. Most Regular Army divisions would train as regiments and then be assembled into full divisions either in France or on the East Coast just prior to departure. Therefore, most of these units did not require the large amount of space that a full 28,000-man division did. Many Regular Army regiments and their support units conducted their training at such unusual places as Syracuse, New York; Gettysburg Battlefield National Park in Pennsylvania; Vancouver Barracks in Washington State; or the Chickamauga National Park in Georgia.

The National Guard and National Army units would require the space and training facilities of the large camps, but it was important to keep the training camps as regionally based as possible to minimize large-scale movements of soldiers around the country. Finally, and perhaps most importantly, the War Department expected the National Army divisions to require a longer training period than the Regular Army or the National Guard divisions.

The time spent on the Mexican border in 1916 and early 1917 had gone a long way to preparing those soldiers for arduous campaigning.

Pvt. 1st Class George Cascio, a native of Italy, served in the Army Air Service from 12 December 1917 until his discharge from the 610th Supply Squadron at the Aviation General Supply Depot, Middletown, Pennsylvania, in March 1919. *New Mexico, World War I Records, 1917–1919*

Conversely, for the National Army divisions, their manpower was to come almost entirely from the draft, meaning the men designated to serve in these units would show up to training camps with no prior military experience. Included in this group were most of the foreign-born men selected in the first draft. This remained the case until the US Army manpower administrators realized that many of the National Guard divisions were undermanned and needed augmentation. Even with consolidation of state units, most Guard divisions were short of manpower. As a result, draftees would very soon find themselves dispatched in large numbers to whichever camp had the greatest manpower need at the moment.

Ultimately, the most important deciding factor of all in camp construction differences turned out to be financial. After receiving the mission to build the thirty-two sites, the Army officers charged with constructing these camps reported that the funding appropriated by Congress for the construction of training camps was enough for only half of the desired camps. Newton Baker wrote:

Because of the impracticability of constructing thirty-two cantonments with the fund appropriated, it was decided, as the National Guard had then in its possession a certain amount of tentage . . . to place the National Guard under canvas that their training might not longer be delayed, and to confine cantonment construction to the sites selected in various divisional areas for the National Army.[2]

As a result of this decision, the National Army divisions would be quartered in more permanent wooden barracks at their training camps. Since these camps were to be more permanent and durable in construction, the sixteen sites chosen were almost entirely in northern or central states. There were a few exceptions to this rule because of the desire for regional training camps: Camps Travis in Texas, Gordon in Georgia, Jackson in South Carolina, and Pike in Arkansas.

Since the soldiers would be living in wooden buildings rather than tents, the National Army camps were officially considered "cantonments." Conversely, the sixteen training sites for the National Guard divisions, being "under canvas," were officially "camps." It was also decided that each camp was to be named after an American soldier or statesman of significance either to the camp's locality or the origin of the soldiers to be trained there. Regardless of the camp/cantonment distinction, all the sites were named Camp Jackson, Camp Meade, Camp Dix, Camp Fremont, etc., as appropriate.

In addition to the soldiers who were to be trained as a division, each camp had a supporting depot brigade. The depot brigade was designed to support the operation of the camp, as well as to serve as a reception station and manpower pool for the divisional units in training. Among the units assigned to the depot brigade were the communications specialists required to maintain the camp's telephone and telegraph system, the camp's firefighting units, the machine shops, the provost guard company, the ordnance depot, and labor battalions. Most important were the reception units, which were to receive the incoming troops and prepare them for their eventual assignment.

Newly arrived men were assigned to the camp's depot brigade for their initial issue of clothing and some rudimentary military instruction before being forwarded to a unit. While often disparagingly referred to as the "Spare Parts Brigade," the depot brigade at each camp served a critical mission.

Each division in training was constantly losing men due to medical disqualification, sickness, or accident, and the depot brigade was designed to quickly provide replacement soldiers. Despite their best efforts, most divisions would still be understrength when the time came to deploy to France, and large groups of untrained or undertrained men were added to the unit at the last minute. Many of these soldiers would be almost straight from the draft boards and would add a training burden on the NCOs of the unit. When these men were foreign born and recent arrivals in the country the burden increased, since it became necessary to translate everything into a language they could understand.

National Army soldiers arriving at their training sites found newly built, two-story wooden barracks awaiting them. The upper floors were large dormitory-style rooms without partitions. Iron cots for the entire company were arranged side by side in long rows, with a designated amount of floor space for each soldier; theoretically, this ensured that sleeping quarters were not too crowded. The lower floor in each of these buildings was divided into two long rooms: one served as a mess hall, including long tables and benches, with a serving counter at the far end. The other room served as an assembly room suitable for indoor training events or as additional living space for assigned soldiers.

Outside each barracks building was a latrine facility with shower stalls and requisite toilets.[3] As Vermont's published history of the war later reported, the "recruit found his camp well equipped to give him every comfort. He was required to work hard but there was little hardship under a system which quartered him in well-heated, well-lighted barracks, and which gave him plenty of wholesome food."[4]

To build so many "cities" as quickly as possible required standardization of building components and camp layouts. The War Department designed a model building that became the basic barrack used across the country. "Walls, windows, doors, even locks and hinges" were standardized for use at all sites.[5]

The basic layout of each National Army training camp also followed a standard pattern in the shape of a giant "U." The barracks and administrative buildings made up the columns, and the divisional headquarters buildings were the bend at the bottom. Rail spurs were to be built down both sides of the "U" to provide fast distribution of supplies and equipment, as well as prepare for the eventual departure of the units. Because of terrain features, some camps were actually more "V" shaped; Camp Travis, Texas, was almost a "Z" shape; and Camp Lee, Virginia, was closer to a "J." Nevertheless, building to the "U" standard was a good plan, and it generally worked well.[6]

The sixteen National Guard training sites differed significantly from the National Army sites in several ways. Beyond the obvious difference in living quarters, there was also the matter of geographic location. With the exception of Camp Fremont in California, the National Guard training camps were below the Mason-Dixon Line. There were three sites in Texas and two each in Alabama, Georgia, and South Carolina. The others were in Southern California, Mississippi, Oklahoma, New Mexico, Louisiana, and North Carolina.

Ferdinando Arrighetti, a tailor from Pisa, Italy, served in a provisional ordnance regiment at Camp McArthur, Texas. Discharged in January 1919, Arrighetti returned to civilian life and became a boilermaker. *New Mexico, World War I Records, 1917–1919*

Francis J. Gurtler, born in Glasgow, Scotland, was living on Electric Avenue in Rochester, New York, when war was declared. He enlisted in the New York National Guard just four days later and, during training at Camp Wadsworth, South Carolina, was assigned to the Sanitary Detachment of the 108th Infantry Regiment. *Courtesy 108th Infantry, NYARNG and NYDMNA*

Since so many Guardsmen had received training along the Mexican border, the War Department reasoned that the Guard divisions should not need as long a training period as the National Army units. Since Guardsmen would train in the South in a milder climate, they did not require more permanent facilities, so the billets for the camps could be constructed more economically using eight-man canvas squad tents. On paper it made perfect sense: shorter training, temporary billets, and better weather equaled significant cost savings. In a time when every penny was strictly allocated and accounted for, this fiscal responsibility was praised. Besides, there was not enough money appropriated to build wooden barracks for the National Guard anyway.

After the camps were finished, a government study found that the cost per soldier to build the National Guard camps was $87.60. The most economically built National Guard camp was Camp Sheridan, Alabama, where the average cost per soldier was only $67.90.[7] In late July 1917, when the camps began to fill with Guard units, everyone was pleased with the prospect of saving so much money.

Focus then turned to other important issues, such as where to find enough weapons, unit equipment, and uniforms for the troops, and enough ships to transport them to France. Unfortunately, the War Department's anticipation of good weather in the South was dashed by the harsh reality of winter 1917–1918. The winter came early, and with it the most severe weather the southern half of the United States had seen in many years. What was expected to be temperate and pleasant weather was instead cold, rainy, and muddy. Men, animals, and machines became stuck in the snow and the mud. The men huddled in their tents and spent their days looking for firewood to feed their stove tents. Ultimately, the only benefit of having the camps in the South was that the weather actually prepared them for what they faced in France in autumn 1918.

Another uniquely crushing blow to the National Guard units after arriving at their camps was the breaking up of old state regimental organizations to make new regiments and brigades. Reorganizing the units was a necessary evil; regiments that had been at full peacetime strength with 2,000 soldiers now needed 3,700 to be complete at "war" strength. Rifle companies that had consisted of 150 men now fielded 250 men.

Isaac Tierson, born in Amsterdam, Holland, was among the first to rally to the flag by joining the New York National Guard just days after declaration of war. Only seventeen at the time, Tierson was assigned to the 108th Infantry Regiment, 27th Division. After training at Camp Wadsworth, South Carolina, the 108th deployed to France on board the impounded and recently renamed USS *Leviathan*. Tierson was killed in action at St. Quentin in September 1918. *Courtesy New York State Archives and the 108th Infantry Regiment, NYARNG*

Soldiers who had served and drilled together for years were suddenly in different units. Many of these manpower shortages would soon be filled with draftees. Originally, there was an attempt to add soldiers from the same general area to these National Guard units, but this quickly became unmanageable; expediency took over, and the nearest manpower pool became the provider.

In some cases, large numbers of men were transferred from one division to another on the basis of schedules of deployment to France. This became a vicious cycle, since some units were repeatedly "harvested" for soldiers and not only depleted in manpower but also moved back in the deployment cycle, leaving them open to even more harvesting. There is little doubt that, especially among National Guard units, the sudden influx of new men, many of whom spoke a different language, led to hard feelings.

One North Dakota Guardsman serving in the 164th Infantry Regiment, 41st Division, commented on the influx of drafted men that disrupted his unit's cohesion by writing that they were a "tough and motley crowd. They did not like the country, the army or us and there was a lot of trouble which continued after we hit France."[8] Another North Dakota officer, Capt. Thomas Thomsen, reported that he had thirteen new men in his company, all with Italian names who "cannot read, write, speak or understand English."[9] In fact, all the units of the 164th were augmented with draftees "of German, Turkish, Austrian and Bulgarian nationality with relatives fighting for the Central Powers." Ironically enough, the 164th would be harvested after arrival in France, and most of the men were sent to become part of the 1st Division.[10]

Animosity between Guardsmen and their new comrades was not limited to native-born and foreign-born soldiers. The augmentation of the 57th Pioneer Infantry Regiment—originally raised from New England National Guardsmen—with a number of southern draftees led to a great deal of enmity. One southerner later wrote that the unit's officers "were a hateful bunch of cusses. . . . They called us Southern Hook Worms. They even kicked some of the boys in the pants."[11] Another Guard unit, the famous 42nd "Rainbow" Division, would take North/South animosity even further and experienced confrontations between New Yorkers of the 165th Infantry Regiment and Alabamans of the 167th Infantry Regiment.[12]

The effect of the influx of foreign-born soldiers on National Army units can be seen in the 82nd Division—ironically nicknamed the "All Americans"—composed

Pvt. 1st Class Frederick J. Utton was born in Brisbane, Australia, and enlisted on 18 August 1917. He was assigned to the 349th Ambulance Company of the 88th Division. A sign of the times during the early period of stateside training, Utton's portrait shows him wearing a campaign hat, canvas leggings, and a very outdated M1903-style service coat. *Courtesy New Mexico, World War I Records, 1917–1919*

of draftees from Georgia, Alabama, and Tennessee and trained at Camp Gordon, Georgia. After six weeks of training together, most of the enlisted men were transferred to National Guard divisions, leaving only a cadre of trainers and a few of the original draftees remaining. As was common during the period, the transferred men were suddenly replaced by large numbers of soldiers from "Camps Devens, Dix, Upton, Lee and Meade, until by November 1, 1917, approximately 28,000 [new] men had entered Camp Gordon."[13] The 82nd's most famous soldier, Alvin York, would record in his diary in February 1918 that "they put me by some Greeks and Italians to sleep. I couldn't understand them and they couldn't understand me, and I was the homesickest boy you have ever seen."[14] York was further dismayed at the inability of the foreign-born soldiers to shoot their rifles. As a mountain-raised farm boy well experienced in long-range shooting, he found "army shooting was tolerably easy for me." He further wrote that:

Greeks and Italians came out on the shooting range and the boys from the big cities. They hadn't been used to handling guns. And sometimes at 100 yards they would not only miss the targets, they would even miss the hills on which the targets were placed.[15]

Arriving in France in May 1918 and now armed with Enfield rifles, York did notice that the foreign-born soldiers were improving, because they "had stayed continuously on the rifle range for a month or two and got so they could shoot well." He even admitted that, although he missed all his fellow Tennessee soldiers, the new guys were also "fairly good pals, too. . . . It sure was a mixed platoon, with the Greeks and Italians and New York Jews, and there were some Irish and one German."[16] In time, York came to appreciate them even more for their aggressive attitudes and wrote:

Those Greeks and Italians and the New York Jews! Ho ho. They didn't want to lie around and do nothing, and they would get on top and get the Germans out. They were always asking, where was the war? They were always ready to go over the top in time of battle, almost too anxious to go over the top.[17]

The model M1917 service coat belonging to Sgt. Hyrant N. Yazujian, a Turkish-born Doughboy. After the war Yazujian lived in Williamsport, Pennsylvania, and operated a barbershop there until his death in December 1948. *Courtesy Joel McConnell*

The historian of the 82nd Division confirmed much of York's comments, writing: "approximately twenty per cent of these [new] men were of foreign birth. . . . Training was seriously handicapped by a substantial percentage of men who were unable to read and write English." The problem was made worse because the:

average American was unable to distinguish between the German or Austrian Pole and the Russian Pole, the Czecho-Slovak or Jugo-Slav. . . . If the soldier was a Greek he might be a partisan of King Constantine or of M. Venizelos [Eleftherios K. Venizelos, a Cretan-born, Greek political leader who sided with the Allies as opposed to the Greek royal family, who were more supportive of the German side due perhaps in some part to King Constantine's German wife]."[18]

Adding to the confusion, many Americans had so little knowledge of the Balkans that in some draft and service records Macedonia was listed randomly as being part of Turkey, Greece, Serbia, or Bulgaria.

Over time, the 82nd managed to rid itself of some of the more serious troublemakers and established English-language classes to help foreign-born soldiers. Most importantly, as York noted, the extra training was doing a good job of honing their soldier skills. Nevertheless, before deploying to France the 82nd Division still discharged some 1,400 enemy aliens as being unsuitable or unreliable for further service.

At the training camps, newly arrived men were usually initially assigned to the camp's depot brigade, where they underwent initial processing and training. In 1918, the initial classification of inductees at Camp Travis was typical of what all soldiers experienced. Called the "Bull Pen" at Camp Travis, the procedure was designed to efficiently receive, examine, and process the large number of men coming in via the draft.

With each step in the process the men were theoretically evaluated for classification in the Army. Throughout this process, each inductee caused a veritable blizzard of paperwork to descend: Forms 1010 P.M.G.O., 1029 P.M.G.O. (A and B), 88 S.G.O. (M.D.), 637 A.G.O., 260 A.G.O., 81 S.G.O., and 22-2 A.G.O., to name only a few. The results of the various exams and interviews were carefully recorded on these forms and became a part of the official personnel file for each soldier.[19]

The typical inductee arrived at camp on a train in the company of dozens of other men from the same local draft board. A cursory medical examination while the men were still aboard the train allowed officers to segregate men with obvious communicable diseases. The healthy men were marched to the receiving station, where another medical exam further thinned the ranks of the newcomers. Soon after this, perhaps as early as the next day, the men were again given a physical examination, during which they were screened for venereal disease and tuberculosis. Follow-on exams largely repeated what each soldier had gone through prior to induction, but also included a neuropsychiatric exam. At the conclusion of these exams, each soldier was found to be either fit or unfit for military service; those deemed fit next moved to the quartermaster's office for issuance of uniform and miscellaneous equipment, including the all-important mess kit.

There followed more personnel and administrative paperwork, including supply slips and finance forms. Here the men were first interviewed as to their education, years of military experience, and desired branch of service. After inoculations the men were assigned to a unit at the camp, perhaps to the depot brigade if the tactical units were already at full manpower. After this, the camp personnel branch submitted a consolidated report to the War Department in Washington, DC, showing the various vocations, special skills, or relevant experience of the new soldiers. Theoretically, this allowed the War Department to collect and collate the reports from each camp and compare the list to vacancies in each unit. The War Department would then submit a levy against each camp, directing them to send certain soldiers with specific required skills to other camps to fill vacancies.

Among other things, reformers in the Progressive Era were known for their efforts to categorize, quantify, and classify. These efforts soon extended to the large number of men drawn into the US Army. By early 1918, psychologists stationed at each Army post began to administer exams to new recruits. The alpha exam was given to literate recruits, while the beta exam was given to men who were illiterate.

On the basis of their scores, the men were put into one of three categories: superior, average, or inferior. Nearly half the whites and about 90 percent of the blacks scored below a mental age of thirteen.[20] Clearly, a large number of men would be considered unfit or marginally fit for military service. The variety of different languages spoken by the recruits exacerbated the problems of training and discipline.

Russian-born, Yiddish-speaking Max Gordon was assigned to the 302nd Ammunition Train of the 77th division. Seen here in a relaxed pose wearing a campaign hat and canvas leggings, Gordon had this portrait made while he was in training at Camp Upton. There were seven Max Gordons drafted from New York State, and four of them were born in Russia. After the war Gordon became a dentist. *Courtesy of Brennan C. Gauthier*

Major E. Alexander Powell, assigned to military intelligence during the war, provided an example of the types of abuse that foreign-born soldiers were subject to, in this case at Camp Gordon:

Private Sobolowski, failing to spell his name, was struck in the jaw by his sergeant, so successfully that the jaw was broken and a few teeth were knocked out. The private went to the hospital and the sergeant to the guard-house, pending court-martial proceedings.

Private Pagarzelski replied to his corporal in Polish, which the corporal considered highly abusive. The private was court-martialed and sixty dollars of his pay was forfeited. As a consequence the man was not only unable to help his aged mother, but was left without a penny for himself.

Private Sznyder, being on guard duty, misunderstood the orders repeated to him by the corporal of the guard, and naturally did not comply with them. As a result he was arrested and put in the guard-house, fifty-seven dollars being taken from him by a corporal, of which only thirty-five dollars was returned. The corporal took advantage of his ignorance of English to appropriate a part of the money.

A Russian was arrested for evasion of military service. After he had spent six weeks in the guard-house it was discovered [through an interpreter] that the man was arrested before he had received notification of being drafted.[21]

These and similar incidents must have been common in the early days of the draft, before the establishment of development battalions and before the War Department implemented measures to assist foreign-born soldiers in early 1918.

In reaction to this problem of undereducated and illiterate soldiers, the Army formed several types of units to accommodate men who, for one reason or another, were unfit for combat or other types of soldierly duties. Development Battalions—one of these types of units—were formed in May 1918, at the direction of the War Department. General Orders Number 45 stated that the battalions were designed:

to relieve divisions, replacement, and other organizations, etc., of unfit men; to conduct intensive training with a view of developing unfit men for duty with combatant or noncombatant forces, either within the United States or for service abroad; to promptly rid the service of all men who, after thorough trial and examination, were found physically, mentally, or morally incapable of performing the duties of a soldier.[22]

Thus, these battalions sprang up at training camps across the United States. By war's end, there had been no less than seventy-eight development battalions active at sixteen camps. There were separate battalions for "white" and "colored" men, and men with venereal disease were further segregated.[23] General Orders Number 45 additionally stated:

When an enlisted man is inapt or does not possess the required degree of adaptability for military service . . . or is an alien enemy or allied alien enemy, or is an alien who is not a declarant and has been drafted through his ignorance of his rights under the Selective Service Law, or any other reason is not fitted to perform the duties of a soldier at home or abroad, his company or detachment commander will report the facts to the commanding officer, who will appoint a board consisting of one officer, preferably the summary court. The board will determine whether or not the soldier should be transferred to the Development Battalion.[24]

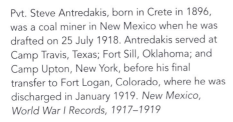

Pvt. Steve Antredakis, born in Crete in 1896, was a coal miner in New Mexico when he was drafted on 25 July 1918. Antredakis served at Camp Travis, Texas; Fort Sill, Oklahoma; and Camp Upton, New York, before his final transfer to Fort Logan, Colorado, where he was discharged in January 1919. *New Mexico, World War I Records, 1917–1919*

Pvt. Adolfo Sartini, born in Italy in 1889, was drafted and reported for duty in March 1918. Sartini was initially assigned to the 2nd Engineer Training Regiment at Camp Humphreys, Virginia, then to the 215th Engineer Regiment in October 1918. Shortly thereafter Sartini succumbed to bronchopneumonia, a secondary infection and common result of having contracted influenza. *Photo and information courtesy Bob Sartini and Ruth Craig*

The issue of soldiers who could not speak English—and there were thousands who could not—was specifically addressed:

> Soldiers who have not sufficient knowledge of the English language to enable them properly to perform their duties may be transferred to the Development Battalions, where instruction to the necessary extent will be imparted.[25]

One can readily see just how important it was for company commanders of depot brigades to pay attention to the adaptability of incoming draftees. Upon them rested the responsibility to determine whether a man was fit for the normal duties of a combat soldier. The War Department's own development battalion training manual states that men were to be transferred into the battalions by reason of the "consideration of a combination of physical and other causes and conditions having to do with education, training, religion, nationality, etc."[26]

Once in a development battalion, men were further classified. They were either:

> a. Clearly unfit for any service, ready for S.C.D. [surgeon's certificate of disability, resulting in a discharge from the service] at once.
>
> b. Needing hospital treatment at once. These are to be transferred to base hospital or to general hospital.
>
> c. To enter such special treatment and training as is provided within the development battalion.[27]

Many of the physically fit foreign-born soldiers fell into the group under letter "c." These men, after training, treatment, and careful observation, were finally classified as follows:

> Class A: fit physically for general military service.
>
> Class B: not quite fit physically for general military service, but free from serious organic disease, able to do an average day's work; able to walk 5 miles, to see and hear well enough for ordinary purposes; able to perform duty equivalent to garrison duty, labor battalion, shop work [in a trade] at home or abroad, or combat service at home [US Guards].
>
> Class C: fit only for duty in selected occupation or in a restricted capacity to which they must be limited.
>
> Class D: physically unfit for any military service.[28]

Just who were the men assigned to development battalions? Ralph V. D. Magoffin, former Army Morale officer, remembered:

Everybody who was sent to [a development battalion] considered himself a derelict, stranded more eternally and to be buffeted more rudely than even a soldier relegated to the Depot Brigade. In our camp was a Development Battalion of 10,000 men, 3,000 of whom could not even speak English. . . . Many men were lame, halt, and blind, and I speak advisedly, because the feet of several pointed backwards, hundreds carried canes and went to their daily exercise so slowly that they were called the Caterpillar Brigade. . . . Many were dropped a class or two in physical qualifications because of venereal disease. Some were white pacifists, some were yellow, and 3,000 were Italians, Poles, Yids, Russians, Armenians, and other foreigners who could not speak English, and seemed not to have the faintest idea of what it was all about. All of them wanted to go home.[29]

Even allowing for hyperbole, we get the impression that these men presented a serious challenge to the Army's training program. Before the creation of development battalions, these men suffered through training in combat units or languished in depot brigades performing menial chores, if they were able to do even that much. Army Field Clerk Will Judy, assigned to Headquarters, 33rd Division at Camp Logan, Texas, watched a group of these men marching to work in January 1918: "The provisional regiment of aliens, weaklings and undesirables marched by in overalls, carrying picks and shovels." Later in April, he watched another group leaving the camp: "Several hundred soldiers who are aliens, departed for Camp Lewis Washington, to be interned there or employed in domestic service during the rest of the war. They marched away with smiling faces, altho a close observation showed that most of the smiles were akin to sneers."[30]

Certainly many men, including foreign-born soldiers, were discharged on a surgeon's certificate of disability (SCD). Many men who were unfit were identified right away and discharged before being assigned to a development battalion. For example, James Aceto, an Italian immigrant, reported for duty at Camp Sherman, Ohio, on 26 August 1918. He served only a few days before his discharge on 7 September for "Physical Disability (flaccid flat feet with abduction and eversion) which existed prior to induction and was not incurred in line of duty." Paul Tenuta, a twenty-three-year-old Italian immigrant, was drafted on 21 July 1918 and sent to Camp Zachary Taylor, Kentucky. One week later, Tenuta was discharged because he was "under weight."[31] Such situations, which must have been numerous both among native-born and foreign-born inductees in summer 1918, must have given medical officers at training camps cause to question the competence of the draft board members and medical examiners who sent such men to the camps.

Another example of the problems encountered at the camps is seen in the example of nine Chinese-born men drafted from the state of Utah. Of the nine, only two of them served overseas; one was Wong Foo, a cook in Company G, 8th Infantry Regiment, 8th Division. The 8th Infantry Regiment was one of the few units from that division that made it overseas just before the armistice; Foo served overseas from 28 October 1918 to 14 July 1919. Sims Kwan, a private in Company M, 308th Infantry

Axel Hawkensen (seen here at left as a sergeant at Fort Douglas, Arizona, in September 1915) was born in 1886, in Sweden, and joined the US Army in 1910 as a private. He was later promoted to first lieutenant during the war. He was still serving as an officer in the Army when he passed away in 1934. *Courtesy John E. Patton*

Regiment, 77th Division, was killed in action on 15 October 1918, during the terrible fighting in the Argonne Forest. One of the remaining seven men who served stateside, Louie Gow, was a member of the 133rd Spruce Squadron, part of the large contingent of military loggers sent to the Pacific Northwest to cut and process lumber used for military aircraft. Another of the stateside soldiers, Yee Wind Dew, served only eight days in the 166th Depot Brigade at Camp Lewis, Washington, in September 1918, before his discharge, probably for medical reasons.[32]

A rudimentary study of New York State abstracts also gives a very clear indication of the incredible diversity of the force being conscripted. There were 89 Australians listed in the New York files, along with 10,214 from Ireland, 3,119 from Poland, 92 from Argentina and Peru, 4 from Honduras, 16 from South Africa, 2,650 from Germany, 89 from Brazil, 11 from New Zealand, 5 from Iceland, 351 from Switzerland, and more than 33,000 from Italy.[33]

Not every man who went into the Army was a novice; some of the men had prior service in the military of their country of origin. Several Indian men had served in the British Army, including Mohammed Hanif, who served for three years as an infantryman in the Ceylonese Army, and a number of Italians had served in Italy's army. In fact, there were so many men in the United States who had served in the Italian Army that, as reported on 2 October 1917 in a Washington, DC, newspaper, the *Evening Star*, thought was given to raising units comprising only Italians.

The premise was that the many former Italian Army officers and NCOs living in the United States could quickly adjust to American Army drills and tactics, then provide leadership for their countrymen. Although the notion of raising strictly Italian units was never seriously contemplated by senior US Army officials, the exact same concept was later applied to the formation of an unusual military unit known as the "Slavic Legion."[34]

There were also some men who had previously served in the US military and were "old soldiers." One of these was Nicholas E. Abbaticchio, who was born near Naples, Italy. He came with his family to Latrobe, Pennsylvania, in the 1870s and joined the Medical Reserve Corps as a first lieutenant on 28 July 1917. A physician, Abbaticchio served throughout the war at Fort Oglethorpe and Camp Wheeler, Georgia, and he was discharged on 13 January 1919. Abbaticchio was also a veteran of the Philippine Insurrection, having enlisted in the Army Hospital Corps in 1899. He served in the Philippines as a hospital steward from 22 December 1899 to 7 August 1902. Abbaticchio's brother, Edward James Abbaticchio, was a well-known major league baseball player for the Philadelphia Phillies and the Pittsburgh Pirates; he was the first known major leaguer of Italian descent.[35]

At America's entry into the war, women were present in the armed forces as commissioned officers in the Army Nurse Corps and Navy Nurse Corps. The US Navy and Marines quickly authorized the recruitment of enlisted women to fill some administrative positions that freed men for combat or sea duty. Army nurses, among them some foreign-born women, distinguished themselves whether they served in the United States or in a combat zone. In the States, many women served in large station hospitals, where they tended sick and wounded soldiers.

The Army recognized the value of Greenwich, England–born William Anderson's seven years in the Scots Greys, an elite British army cavalry unit. As a result, they promoted him to second lieutenant and sent him to Camp Lee, Virginia, to train other soldiers. *Courtesy Genesee County, Michigan, Archives*

Among the foreign-born nurses in the Army were two ladies from New Zealand: Blanche S. Hadlund and Kittie Zacharaiah. Nurse Hadlund had the misfortune to serve at Camp Devens Base Hospital during the very worst of the Spanish flu epidemic, while Nurse Zacharaiah served with Base Hospital #3 in New York City before deploying to Vauclaire, France, in early 1918.[36]

First Lt. Lillian J. Ryan, a native of Ireland, served as chief nurse at the base hospital at Camp Merritt, New Jersey. First Lt. Reba G. Cameron, a native of Nova Scotia, Canada, was chief nurse at the general hospital at Plattsburg Barracks, New York, in 1918. After the war she served in the same capacity at the general hospital in Hampton, Virginia. As chief nurse, Cameron "was an example and an inspiration to her entire staff, and was in large measure responsible for the success of these special hospitals."[37]

With the signing of the armistice on 11 November 1918, and notwithstanding the necessity of providing an army of occupation to serve in Germany, the US Army began to demobilize. Such a huge task had to be accomplished systematically; the first men to leave the service were of necessity recent inductees who were undergoing training. It would be important to retain a cadre of men in stateside camps to allow for the reception and processing of the roughly two million men from overseas who would soon be returning and awaiting discharge.

On 15 November 1918, the War Department issued an order to begin demobilizing the development battalions; these "unfit" soldiers were then among the first to receive their discharge.[38]

To understand the experience of a typical foreign-born soldier assigned to a development battalion we will look at a sample of thirty-nine such men drawn from the neighboring Wisconsin cities of Kenosha and Racine. These two cities can be considered typical midwestern industrial cities of

Posing for a picture at Camp Dix, New Jersey, is Andre Gryp, a Belgian-born Doughboy. Gryp first served with the 153rd Depot Brigade and then the 310th Infantry Regiment, 78th Division. He was killed in action on 20 October 1918 at Bois des Loges, during the Meuse-Argonne Offensive, and is buried in the American Cemetery at Romagne-sous-Montfaucon. *Courtesy Rochester and Monroe County, New York*

that time, with a good mix of native-born and immigrant men. The cities had factories, tanneries, and rail yards, and they were about sixty to eighty miles north of Chicago, making them an important link between Chicago and the northwestern prairies.[39] The native countries of the men were Italy (17), Armenia/Turkey (8), Russia (5), Greece (3), Poland (2), Denmark (2), Belgium (1), and Sweden (1).

Since most men were sent to a training camp on induction, their camp of assignment generally reflects their midwestern geographic location. Men were transferred among various camps, and an immigrant soldier could be assigned to a development battalion anywhere along the way. Of the men above, most went to Camp Taylor, Kentucky; Camp McClellan, Alabama; or Camp Grant, Illinois. It should be noted that some went as far as Texas or Massachusetts. The occupation followed by the men in this sample is typical of the overall US immigration pattern, with more men in unskilled or semiskilled positions than in skilled or professional positions. By far, the largest category was laborer, with seventeen, followed by painter with three and foundry worker and shoemaker with two each.

Many of the men in this sample were physically unfit to assume the duties of a soldier. Reviewing the service cards for the foreign-born soldiers in this sample, we find the following:

Nels P. Boye, a thirty-year-old native of Denmark serving in the 3rd Development Battalion, Camp Zachary Taylor, Kentucky, served two months before being discharged with a scrotal hernia and is listed as 10 percent disabled.

Victor Buisse, a twenty-seven-year-old native of Belgium, was transferred from the 344th Infantry Regiment, 86th Division, to a development battalion at Camp Grant in fall 1918. In October 1918, he was discharged with a 50 percent disability, suffering from a "constitutional psychopathic inferiority."

Leo Chobanian, a thirty-one-year-old native of Armenia serving in a development battalion, was discharged on an SCD five days after the armistice. Chobanian suffered from "chronic myocardity."

Samie Hateras was a twenty-four-year-old native of Greece serving in the 5th Development Battalion at Camp MacArthur, Texas, when he was discharged on an SCD because he suffered from "tuberculosis, pulmonary, chronic, arrested."

Peter Plovitz, a twenty-four-year-old native of Russia serving in a Camp Custer development battalion, was discharged in September 1918 after serving about five months. Due to "mental deficiency, imbecility," Plovitz was given a 2 percent disability rating.

The constant transferring and shuffling of men between units and camps did nothing to help the foreign-born soldier learn and assimilate. The case of Giacinto Fumo (also spelled Furno), a twenty-nine-year-old Italian immigrant, illustrates the challenges faced by these men and by their commanding officers, who struggled to assemble and train an effective fighting force.

Fumo, who had thirty-three months of prior service in the Italian army, was drafted and reported for duty in November 1917. He was sent to Camp Custer, where he was assigned to the 340th Infantry Regiment, 85th Division. On 15 December 1917, Fumo was caught in a mass transfer to Camp Pike, Arkansas, as part of the 345th Infantry Regiment, 87th Division. He was probably having trouble adapting; on 1 June 1918, Fumo was transferred to the 162nd Depot Brigade at Camp Pike. On 18 June, Fumo was transferred again, this time to Company A, 19th Battalion, United States Guards at "Camp Stallis." The US Guards were units made of men who were fit for guard duty but not fit for active combat service; many of the men in US Guards battalions were foreign-born men who had served in development battalions. But Fumo was in for one more transfer, this time on 4 August to the 3rd Development Battalion, 165th Depot Brigade at Camp Travis. There he served until his discharge on 7 December 1918. It is clear to see from this example that in an effort to find a place for someone to serve effectively, men were sometimes shunted around almost aimlessly.

At the time of their induction into the service, at least eighteen of the men in the sample were aliens, ten were declarants, one was a naturalized citizen, and the status of ten others is unknown. Eighteen of the men became citizens while in the Army. At least six others became citizens after their tour of duty.

There were other units created for men who, for one reason or another—including lack of ability with the English language—were unfit for active combat service. Among those were the United States Guards Battalions and Limited Service Regiments. Foreign-born soldiers, whether in combat, combat support, or other units, were a large part of the newly forming National Army.

All things considered, and in spite of the many problems caused by the breaking up of old units, the occasional animosity between northerners and southerners, and the massive influx of foreign-born troops, the divisions continued to train as best they could, knowing that soon it might be their turn to deploy to France.

Grudgingly at first, the training cadres drilled the men as best they could while continually having to start over with new men and new officers. Even the soldiers slowly began to develop camaraderie that lasted well after their soldiering days were over. After the war, many would look back on their training period with some sense of humor and accomplishment. For some foreign-born soldiers there would be one more hurdle to cross before they could join their comrades on the journey to the Western Front.

## CHAPTER FOUR

# NATURALIZATION AND DEPLOYMENT

:

We welcome you to a land of equal opportunity, freedom of speech, political and religious liberty. – Judge Henry D. Clayton, US District Court[1]

For 1,000 years our forefathers have been subject to the tyrant's rule. . . . We have been allowed to come here . . . and enjoy the privilege of this great nation. We would indeed be ungrateful if we did not offer it our services in the time of its greatest need. – Sgt. Rudi Nan, 112th Trench Mortar Battery, 37th Division[2]

All large-scale military deployments are perfect opportunities for things to go wrong, usually at the worst possible moment. Many units with foreign-born soldiers were about to find that out firsthand when it came time to deploy to France. Despite the provision to exempt enemy aliens from the draft, many of them, either through negligence or confusion, were inducted and sent to camp. After the initial draft of September and October 1917, "it was found that somewhat less than 1,000 German alien nondeclarants were reported by the boards as having been sent to camp; the number of German declarants sent to camps was also doubtless an appreciable one."[3] The US declaration of war against Austria-Hungary on 11 November 1917 resulted in the immediate reclassification of about 9,000 nondeclarant Austro-Hungarian US soldiers as enemy aliens. Most of these men had waived their right to exemption, and the provost marshal later concluded that "large numbers, in fact a great majority of these men were of the oppressed races of Austro-Hungary and therefore sympathetic with the cause of the allies and ready to remain in camp."[4]

The status of soldiers from Turkey and Bulgaria proved to be another special case late in the war. Although technically, and for purposes of the draft, these men were enemy aliens, their precise status awaited determination by the US State Department. On 24 October 1918, after thousands of Turks, Armenians, and Bulgarians

After induction into the Army in August 1918, Italian-born Pasquale D'Alessandro received training at Camp Greenleaf, Georgia. On completion, D'Alessandro was assigned to Base Hospital Number 1 in Vichy, in the Intermediate Section. A shoe designer by trade, he was one of the cofounders of the I Miller Shoe Company. *Courtesy Robert Dalessandro*

had already been inducted, the State Department held that these men were enemy aliens, "but before instructions could be published carrying into effect the decision of the department, hostilities against Turkey and Bulgaria were suspended and the instructions not promulgated."[5]

One of the first units to run into a major problem with "enemy aliens" in their ranks was the 37th Division, composed mainly of Ohio National Guardsmen and organized at Camp Sheridan. Months of training had been completed and most of the subordinate units of the "Buckeye Division" had been brought up to strength. The final round of physical exams was conducted and the weeding out of those still unfit physically to deploy was completed.

Everyone in the 37th was going full speed in preparation for departure from Camp Sheridan when it happened: a War Department edict that "no subject of a country at war against the allies could be taken overseas." This single statement "disqualified hundreds of men who had volunteered in good faith."[6] It was a devastating blow to the 37th. Large numbers of foreign-born men from Germany and the Austro-Hungarian Empire who had enlisted in Ohio National Guard units were now disqualified from deploying due to the ruling.

The 37th's official history further noted that a good number of these soldiers had served in the Ohio National Guard for a while and:

> were non-commissioned officers. Company H of the 145th Infantry Regiment had enlisted two score or more Bohemians; many of them were sergeants and corporals. . . . The 112th Trench Mortar Battery was composed entirely of Rumanians, born in Transylvania, and—like the Bohemians—former subjects of the Austro-Hungarian Empire.[7]

Making this all the more poignant was the fact that many of these men had voluntarily joined the Guard and probably would not have been drafted or compelled to serve in the US armed forces. Nevertheless, with no recourse whatsoever, the unit commanders in the 37th withdrew these soldiers from training. While the rest of the division was on the rifle range, the now-undeployable "enemy aliens" were assigned to packing and crating divisional equipment for overseas shipment.

Fortunately for all concerned, on 9 May 1918, Congress passed a law allowing "expeditious naturalization" of foreign-born men who were serving in the US Army "during the time the country is engaged in the present war." The law granted the waiving of residency requirements for alien servicemen wanting to become US citizens. They would no longer have to appear in court, file a Declaration of Intention, and reside in the United States five years before taking the oath of allegiance.

Now a serviceman was required to have only two witnesses who could attest to the man's loyalty and a certificate of naturalization would be issued. This law also included soldiers from enemy countries. When news of the legislation reached the stateside training camps, the 37th Division was the first to take advantage of it. The Act of Naturalization procedure and ceremony, along with recognizing the patriotism and service of these soldiers, also had a pragmatic and legal purpose. It ensured that, if captured, these newly minted US citizens could not legally (by international law) be forced into serving in enemies' armies. This was an extremely important point because many of the foreign-born Doughboys in the 37th had come either from Germany or the Austro-Hungarian Empire.

Born in Russia in 1895, Stanley Guba was inducted into the US Army in June 1918; less than thirty days later he was in France, assigned to the 51st Pioneer Infantry Regiment. After serving in the Army of Occupation in Germany, Guba was discharged in August 1919 with a surgeon's certificate of disability rating of 40 percent. *Courtesy NYDMNA*

The world of 1918 was fraught with many dangers in addition to German bullets and the flu. Amadeo Steo was born in Rovigno, Italy, and came to the United States in 1912. He trained at Camp Upton and Camp Dix. Steo and others of his unit were loaded on the HMS *Otranto* and sailed for Liverpool in September 1918. The *Otranto* sank after colliding with another British troop ship, the HMS *Kashmir*. Steo was among the 351 American soldiers who died in the accident. His body was never recovered. *Courtesy Rochester and Monroe County, New York*

Moving quickly, 37th Division staff arranged for a judge and court officials to be brought to the camp on 20 May. At sunrise the next day, the examiners and the applicants came face to face. The senior official, Judge Henry Clayton of the US District Court, was seated with the 37th Division commander on a raised platform. The prospective citizens were marched by their unit officers to a spot in front of the judge. Each soldier in turn was asked questions by Judge Clayton. The unit officers then testified to the Army service and loyalty of the soldier. After each soldier in the unit had been questioned and confirmed, the men marched to a nearby holding area. Another group then appeared in front of the judge to undergo the same procedure.

After the last man was examined, the entire group was formed into a single formation and took the oath of allegiance. Given the chance to speak to the assembled group, Judge Clayton reminded them of their duty and said, "unto you and your heirs forever we grant full fellowship."[8] Speaking on behalf of the new citizens was one of their own, Sgt. Rudi Nan of the 112th Trench Mortar Battery, who said:

> Through you, honorable judge and you, our commanding officer, we express to the government of the United States our appreciation, not only for this wonderful opportunity to so easily become citizens, but also for the privilege of serving side by side with the native sons of America.[9]

Six months later, as the 37th was undergoing a crucible of fire in the Argonne, the reader can wonder how many of these same new Americans still believed that their citizenship had been "easily" obtained.

The newly naturalized citizens were then marched to a waiting train and rejoined their units for movement to port. That first morning at Camp Sheridan, Judge Clayton presided over 366 naturalizations. The next day the process was repeated, and another 297 US citizens were created. By the time he finished, Judge Clayton had officiated

Born in Aintab, Turkey, Hagop N. Chopourian was an ethnic Armenian working in Erie, Pennsylvania, when he was drafted. In this picture, most likely taken in the States during training, he shows off his British-style gas mask while striking a bold pose. Later, after serving in the Meuse-Argonne Offensive, his camera poses will be much less dramatic.

Pvt. Frank (Macileo) Miceli, born in Italy in 1892, was living in Chicago when he was inducted in September 1918. He served in the 14th Company, 161st Depot Brigade, at Camp Grant, Illinois, until his discharge in December 1918. *Courtesy of Beverly Alexandria-Adamski*

over 1,100 naturalizations, and the 37th was extremely grateful to get their men back into its ranks. As the 37th later recorded, when discussing these soldiers, "all of them were to later prove themselves among the best soldiers in the division."[10]

After the war, Ohio published a complete list of every soldier, sailor, and Marine who was credited to the state. A quick scan of the names and birthplaces reveals a wide variety of origins. On one page in sequence there are Gustav Jaimeo, Greece; Russell Jaite, Cleveland; Joe Jajczyk, Russia; Peter Jak, Austria; Joe Jakabek, Austria; Telesfor Jackaczi, Borkij, Poland; Felix Jacala, Cleveland; Frank Jakenovech, Russia; and Daniel Jakeok, Austria. Of these, all served honorably except Peter Jak, who deserted from his Ohio National Guard unit in July 1917.[11]

Another section included Kappele (Canada) serving in the 322 Field Artillery; Kaprovlias (Greece) in the 331st Infantry; Kapuscensky (Poland) in the 119th Field Artillery; three Kapusniaks (all from Poland) serving in the 51st Infantry, 59th Infantry, and the 12th Machine Gun Battalion; two Kapustas (one from Austria-Hungary, the other from Poland) serving in the 383rd Infantry and the 68th Infantry; Karadjas (Turkey) in the 112th Engineers; Karafotis and Karagianis (both from Greece) in the 331st Infantry; and Karamane (Greece) in the 60th Pioneer Infantry Regiment. Serving in the 158th Depot Brigade at Camp Sherman were Karacek (Poland), Karadjoff (Macedonia), Karaffe (British Empire), and Karaklanian (Turkey).[12]

Other divisions, such as the 29th, which was raised from National Guard units of Virginia, Maryland, Delaware, New Jersey, and the District of Columbia, were drawn from much less diverse populations. By the time the 29th was ready to deploy to France, it too had been augmented by a large number of cobelligerent and enemy aliens. Therefore, like the 37th Division, the 29th had to complete the final step needed to integrate these men into the service. On 28 May 1918, the same Judge Clayton began the two-day process of officiating over the administrative procedure for turning almost 800 soldiers of the 29th division into naturalized citizens. There were another perhaps equal number of aliens added to the division too recently to have the necessary affidavits and paperwork completed for naturalization. It was determined that this second group of soldiers would deploy with the 29th Division to France without the "protection" of being naturalized US citizens. It was hoped that

Wearing a bemused smile and a collar disk indicating service in Company F of the 51st Pioneer Infantry Regiment, John Felix Gradek poses in Germany in early 1919. Born in Poland in 1887, Pvt. Gradek was living in Buffalo, New York, when he was inducted into the Army. Unlike his 51st Pioneer Infantry Regiment comrade Stanley Guba (seen in an earlier photograph), Gradek had almost two complete months of military service before arriving in France in July 1918. *Courtesy NYDMNA*

there would be time for them to complete the naturalization process while serving there.[13]

The National Army divisions had the same problem as the National Guard. At Camp Zachary Taylor, the National Army training camp on the outskirts of Louisville, Kentucky, the naturalization ceremony was conducted under the shade of a giant North American ash, which became known as the "Naturalization Tree." That men were eager to avail themselves of this opportunity at Camp Taylor is evident from a partial index of naturalizations for 14 and 15 August 1918, showing a total of 240 immigrant soldiers who applied for and received US citizenship.

In October 1918, three naturalization ceremonies were conducted under the tree, and more than 2,000 men received citizenship. The first of these ceremonies, held on 2 October 1918, was for 400 men representing seventeen countries. Included in that group was Gilmore J. Gayle. Gayle, a native of Kingston, Jamaica, was the first black foreigner to receive US citizenship at Camp Taylor. Gayle graduated from the Field Artillery Course and received an officer's commission to serve in the 814th Pioneer Infantry Regiment.[14]

We can get an idea of the impact this had on immigrant communities by examining the case of men from two neighboring southern Italian villages: Marano Marchesato and Marano Principato. Of the 106 men who were born in one of these villages (or in the immediate environs) and served in the US military during the war, most were aliens at the time of their enlistment. A few either were naturalized citizens or had derived US citizenship through their father. Of the remainder (perhaps ninety to one hundred men), at least forty-three, and probably more, became US citizens while in the service or shortly thereafter, using the provisions of the May 1918 Naturalization Act. A few did so after their return from overseas and before discharge or immediately thereafter.[15]

Some men had begun the process of naturalization before entering the military, and once the law went into effect they were able to expeditiously complete their naturalization. Carmine Chiappetta had declared his intention to become a citizen in

1917; he completed the process a few months after his discharge in 1919. Eugenio Ferraro declared his intention in April 1918; he joined the US Navy soon thereafter and took the oath of allegiance while in the navy in July 1918. Both Carmine Belmonte, who had enlisted just prior to his eighteenth birthday, and Joe Covelli, who was seriously wounded while serving with the 18th Infantry Regiment, 1st Division, in the Meuse-Argonne Offensive, completed their naturalizations after their discharge in 1919.

At Camp Grant, the National Army training site near Rockford, Illinois, federal judge Kennesaw Mountain Landis gave a patriotic speech and then naturalized 800 foreign-born soldiers in August 1918. Landis—the father of Reed Landis, one of the AEF's top scoring fighter pilots—later became the commissioner of Major League Baseball after the 1919 "Black Sox" World Series scandal.[16]

The naturalization procedure was repeated many times at almost every training site to prepare the units for departure to France. Perhaps one of the most interesting naturalization ceremonies took place at Camp Upton, New York, presided over by Maj. Gen. J. Franklin Bell. On this occasion over 300 soldiers took the oath. This total included "13 Austrians, 4 Germans, 2 Mexicans, 1 Montenegrin, 1 Portugese, 24 Turks [and] 25 were negro infantrymen of the 367th Regiment."[17] It is important to reiterate that it was not just European foreign-born men who were registered and inducted; immigrants and resident aliens from all countries were being added to the force.

While the process of induction was fairly uniform across races, follow-on actions were not. White soldiers, and in most cases Asian soldiers, on completion of some period of training would find themselves being sent to any of the Regular Army, National Army, or National Guard units. Men from Haiti, Trinidad, Jamaica, the West Indies, or any of the African nations and considered "colored" would be sent to training locations that supported the African American units of the Army. These units included the two African American combat divisions (the

Pvt. Jerry John Dynek poses for a picture at Camp Funston, Kansas, where he and his 341st Machine Gun Battalion, 89th Division, comrades were trained. A sign of the time, the Bohemia-born Dynek is armed with an obsolete model M1898 Krag-Jørgensen rifle. After the war Dynek returned to his former occupation as a painter.

This postcard, written in Greek by Christos Theoharis, a Salamis, Greece-born soldier at Camp Meade, Maryland, tells his friend Savas Kounas, "With heartfelt wishes I wish that the New Year 1918 be Auspicious, Happy and Healthy. Hope we will meet soon." If the clever poem and picture of Army camp life on the front were not enough, Christos adds "In the Army Camp 29 December 1917." Christos served as a sergeant in a development battalion.

92nd and 93rd), some Pioneer Infantry Regiments (801 through 816), or one of the many labor battalions.

Returning to the overall process of registration and naturalization, there was still a problem remaining to be handled. What made the whole "deploying/not deploying" process even more painful to all the participants was the unforeseen consequence of the Army's strategy, or lack thereof, for providing men to fill each of the combat divisions to their required strength.

At times seeming to defy logic, divisions in training would be directed to select a certain number of their assigned soldiers or recently arrived draftees and to transfer them to another camp. This levy, or "draft" of men, would then fill a unit there to its required strength. Some units, such as the 86th Division, were filled and emptied several times to provide men for other units, each time causing the losing unit's cadre to restart the training process with new arrivals.

This severely affected unit cohesion and training, especially for foreign-born soldiers with language or literacy problems who might be inclined to generally struggle with the whole process. For the receiving units, this influx of troops also proved a mixed blessing. The 33rd Division, undergoing training at Camp Logan near Houston, Texas, provides an illustrative point. Toward the end of 1917, the 33rd Division, composed originally of Illinois National Guard units and under the command of Maj. Gen. George Bell, received notification that they would soon be leaving for France. As a result, Gen. Bell traveled to France for a battlefield tour and coordination meeting to prepare for the 33rd's deployment.

The division was also notified that they would soon receive 3,500 drafted men to bolster their ranks. This was important, because at that time, the 33rd had only some 24,000 of their required 28,000 troops. Adding to the problem was the fact that of their 24,000 soldiers, almost 2,000 either were "enemy" aliens (and therefore at this time unable to deploy) or were in the process of being discharged due to disability. Unfortunately, the promised 3,500 men had not yet arrived some eleven weeks after notification. When Gen. Bell returned from his pre-deployment visit to the front lines in France, he found the division no more ready to deploy than before he left, and his manpower shortage still stood at 4,000. To add to the woes of the 33rd, its artillery brigade received orders to transfer all senior field artillerymen to Fort Sill, Oklahoma, for further training. The division was also ordered to dispatch an infantry regiment to the port of Galveston to provide security for oil storage facilities.

By February 1918, the 33rd Division was still at Camp Logan, and its manpower situation had worsened: shortages had reached the 6,000 mark. Despite these aggravations, Bell continued to train his troops as best he could. When the 33rd, like other divisions, received notification that enemy aliens could now be accepted in the ranks if they were naturalized, it corrected a small part of the manpower problem.

Bell continued to write the War Department, demanding more men for his unit, until finally in April the dam burst and a steady flow of soldiers to Camp Logan began. Starting on 5 April, 2,500 soldiers from Camp Grant began to arrive, followed by 2,300 from the 88th Division at Camp Dodge, Iowa, and another 1,000 from the 84th Division at Camp Taylor. With the arrival of another 1,000 soldiers from Camp Grant on 29

April, the 33rd Division was finally up to strength, having received over 7,100 soldiers in just twenty-four days.

The negative aspect of this influx was obvious; the amount of training these men had received ranged from "some" to "absolutely none." Of particular note is the fact that of the 7,100 soldiers assigned to the 33rd, there were 704 enemy aliens who refused to accept the naturalization process and were transferred, under escort, to Camp Lewis, Washington. The 33rd, at this point almost up to strength, was now ready to deploy. Moving in large trainloads, the units of the 33rd headed eastward toward the transit camps and ports. By 4 June 1918, the division was in France.[18]

In the case of the 79th Division, undergoing training at Camp Meade, Maryland, more than 95,000 men were sent to the post for training. Of those, only 27,000 would

Representing the many thousands of men naturalized at Camp Zachary Taylor, Kentucky, this group of eighteen soldiers originated from fifteen different countries. *Courtesy Camp Zachary Taylor Historical Society, Louisville, Kentucky*

actually deploy in late June 1918 with the 79th; making the situation worse, some 15,000 of these were men who had just arrived in early June and were almost completely untrained. Nevertheless, when the orders came to the 79th to move they saluted and moved, all the while knowing that 58 percent of their soldiers had only "mere rudiments of a military education."[19] The Western Front would prove to be a rough finishing school. The 79th's casualty lists would reflect the cost of their education, but first, like all deploying units leaving their training camps, they had one more stop: the transit camps.

The US Army sent units to a transit camp and port of embarkation on the basis of geographic origin of the unit deploying. Officially there were three camps designated as transit camps to support the movement of Doughboys to France: Camp Mills (Garden City, New York), Camp Merritt (Dumont, New Jersey), and Camp

The certificate of naturalization for Livio L. A. Ciarletta, an Italian-born soldier stationed at Camp Hancock, Georgia. Unlike many of the other foreign-born Doughboys, Ciarletta appears to have been literate and signed his name with a flourish.

Stuart (Newport News, Virginia). The three camps were built specifically to facilitate and direct the movement of soldiers and their units through the seaports and on to transport ships. As time progressed, some training was conducted at these sites, as well as final inventory and inspection of soldiers' equipment prior to embarking for France.

Camp Merritt, fifteen miles northwest of Jersey City, was built to support the passage of troops through the nearby port of Hoboken. Merritt was garrisoned by 6,000 soldiers and could support 38,000 troops at a time.[20] Camp Mills was originally built to support the deployment of the 42nd "Rainbow" Division in September 1917, and then the 41st Division in October 1917. After these two divisions deployed, the camp was closed but was then reopened in April 1918, to support the massive movement of troops through the port of Hoboken when Camp Merritt facilities were overwhelmed.[21]

Camp Stuart, in Virginia, supported the movement of soldiers through the port of Newport News. The camp contained almost 500 buildings, including 296 enlisted and 21 officer barracks, and was capable of housing 18,000 soldiers at a time.[22]

In a country that was truly mobilizing for war, even the nation's colleges and universities played a role. Across the

Eastern Europe had been the home of many of the immigrants coming to the United States in the early twentieth century. As a result, many of the men, such as Romanian-born George Tate, seen here in his Army Model 1917 service coat, soon found themselves serving in the US military. Tate served in the US Army Medical Corps.
*Courtesy John Adams-Graf Collection*

One of the most exotic birthplaces reported by any of the "selected" men was that of Mohammed B. Abdallah, who listed the city of Timbuctoo, in the Sahara Desert, as his birthplace. Ironically, while obviously a Muslim, Pvt. 1st Class Abdallah listed Mohammed as his "Christian" name. A further irony is that Abdallah, a man from the open spaces and clear skies of the Sahara Desert, would spend the war working at a recruit training camp in Syracuse, one of America's most overcast cities. *Courtesy New York State Abstracts of World War I Military Service, 1917–1919*

country, colleges began to conduct specialized military training. Some were charged with developing Reserve Officer Training Corps (ROTC) programs, while others trained men in some of the many specialized skills for which there was no equivalent training available at the thirty-two divisional camps. This program soon came to be known as the Students' Army Training Corps (SATC).

SATC training included everything from basic leadership skills to radio equipment repair and maintenance of large mechanized vehicles. The SATC started in September 1918, with units at many colleges; its purpose was "to utilize effectively the plant, equipment, and organization of the colleges for selecting and training officer candidates and technical experts for service in the existing emergency."[23]

While the typical immigrant might not have the educational background or the wherewithal to attend college, many did, and examples of their participation in the SATC are well documented. For example, on 10 October 1918, Pvt. Orgario Abbadini, a twenty-one-year-old native of Pedaso, Italy, and resident of Fairbanks, Pennsylvania, enlisted in Section A (Collegiate) of the SATC at Bethany College, West Virginia.[24]

Some foreign-born men possessed language skills that came in handy for the US Army. Leopold Meyer was born in Paris, France, in 1887, and served in the French army before arriving in the United States. After the United States entered the war, Meyer "offered [his] services four times, in vain, and finally succeeded in entering

Two Danish-born soldiers inducted from Faribault County, Minnesota: Jens C. Jensen and Knud Hansen. Jensen (left), from Hvilson, Denmark, trained at Camp Wadsworth, South Carolina, and then went to France as a member of the 3rd Pioneer Infantry Regiment. Hansen, from Allinge, Denmark, served at Camp Forrest and Camp Dodge. *Courtesy Faribault County, Minnesota*

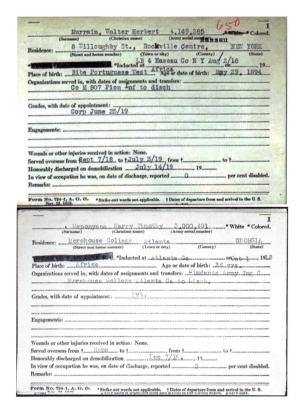

Here are war service cards for two African men: the upper, for Walter H. Murrain; the lower, for Pvt. Harry Timothy Maponyane. Murrain, born in Portuguese, West Africa (today Angola), was assigned to the 807th Pioneer Infantry Regiment and served in France for eleven months. Pvt. Maponyane was a thirty-six-year-old native of Africa who enlisted in the Students' Army Training Corps while studying at Morehouse College. *Murrain card Courtesy New York State Abstracts of World War I Military Service, 1917–1919. Maponyane card courtesy Georgia Archives*

the service of the US Army" in August 1918. After that Meyer must have come to the attention of officers fairly quickly:

> I was voluntarily inducted in the service, and stationed at Fort Sam Houston, San Antonio, Texas, as private in the Corps of Intelligence Police, Southern Department. Made sergeant on August 28th. Was assigned to work the "German activities and propaganda," until September 6th, when I was transferred to Galveston, Texas, to pursue the same work. While on duty in Galveston, gave more of my attention to the German spy work, and remained "under cover" at all times. Was then transferred to Nogales, Arizona, on October 26th. Was assigned to the "military information branch" of our service, work which I pursued until I was finally discharged [at Nogales, 19 March 1919]. My knowledge of French, Spanish, and German helped me greatly all through my service in the Army.[25]

The war ended just as the United States was preparing to send many more divisions to France; this caught the Army with many soldiers in the midst of training or preparing for deployment. Some of these men almost made it to France. Clelio Enriquez, a Mexican-born immigrant living in New Mexico, was drafted in late

The long arm of the draft reached all the way to the Hawaiian Islands, and this Doughboy, unidentified except for being Chinese, found himself in an Army uniform. In all probability, this soldier would have transited from Hawaii to a stateside training base through Fort McDowall on Angel Island in San Francisco Bay. *Courtesy Aaron Pollick*

August 1918 and was sent to Camp Pike, Arkansas. While there, he took advantage of the new naturalization law and became a citizen. After training at Camp Pike, Enriquez "went to Camp Upton, then boarded transport for France was out at sea two days when transport was ordered back on account of the signing of the armistice, from Camp Upton went direct to Camp Cody [New Mexico] where discharge was made."[26]

Immigrants voluntarily enlisted or were drafted right up to the end of the war. A large batch of draftees from Racine, Wisconsin, were called to report for duty on 10 November 1918, one day before the armistice. Among those were several immigrants, including Max Stoll, a twenty-year-old printer from Lithuania, and Frederick Stovring, a thirty-three-year-old tailor from Denmark. Both Stoll and Stovring, along with many others, were sent to Camp Logan, Texas, where they were discharged two days later, unneeded because of the armistice.[27]

For the two million Doughboys in France, that armistice was still a long way off. Before they could think about being demobilized, they first had to survive the very cold winter of 1917–1918, the German Summer Offensive, the St. Mihiel Campaign, a deadly wave of Spanish flu, and, ultimately, the largest battle in American history: the Meuse-Argonne Offensive. When their labors were through, there would be another list of famous names and places in American military history: Cantigny, Belleau Wood, the Rock of the Marne, Blanc Mont Ridge, the "Lost Battalion," and the Hindenburg Line.

:
:

## CHAPTER FIVE

# OVER THERE:
## *Combat Service in France*

:
:

The quickest route to peace is by employing the maximum effort and every possible facility to the fullest extent at the earliest possible moment.[1]

On 28 May 1917, Gen. Pershing left New York City for France on the USS *Baltic*. Accompanying him were 191 members of his staff. It was an inauspicious start for what many Allied leaders had hoped would be a rapid flood of American soldiers. Nevertheless, it was a start. Pershing and his staff made the most of the time at sea, holding numerous planning sessions wherever they could find room on the ship. On reaching England, the Americans met with British staff officers to discuss future liaison and coordination efforts. Following a short cross-channel voyage, they repeated the process with French officers.

For the first US combat division to be organized in France, Pershing had chosen four Regular Army infantry regiments (the 16th, 18th, 26th, and 28th) and the 6th Field Artillery Regiment. Unfortunately, these units were Regular Army in name only. By the time they reached the port of embarkation, many of their trained soldiers had been sent

Born in Oulu, Finland, in March 1895, Ivar Savaloja was a mill worker in Astoria, Oregon, when he was inducted into the Army. Savaloja served in Company E, 38th Infantry Regiment, 3rd Division, and is buried in the National Cemetery in Los Angeles.

to other units to act as cadre, and their places had been filled with many untrained recruits. On 8 June 1917—trained or not—they sailed for France to join Pershing. During the course of the next few months Pershing would receive two more artillery regiments, an engineer regiment, and the other, smaller support units required to complete a division.

As a result of their early deployment, these soldiers would forever have the honor of being the 1st Division, although for most of the twentieth century they would be better known by their nickname: "The Big Red One."[2]

Two National Guard divisions (the 26th and the 42nd) and the 2nd Division (formed in France from Regular Army and Marine Corps units) soon followed. The 26th was a combination of National Guard units from all the New England states and was proudly known as the "Yankee" Division. That said, it would be George Dilboy, a man born in a Greek-occupied section of Turkey, who would become the iconic symbol of the Yankee Division's bravery in combat.

German-born Cpl. Bernard H. Hahnke served in Headquarters Company of the 5th Regiment of Marines, 4th Brigade, 2nd Division. Hahnke enlisted in the Marine Corps in May 1917, and this picture appears to have been taken shortly after his arrival in France. *Courtesy Steve Girard*

While the 42nd was known as the "Rainbow" Division for its inclusion of Guard units from twenty-six states and the District of Columbia, its New York contribution—the 165th Infantry Regiment—was also a diverse group. Among the ranks were twenty-three men from Ireland, as well as representatives from France, the West Indies, Sweden, the Netherlands, Scotland, Canada, and Russia. A number of these would make the ultimate sacrifice, including Pvt. John (James) Farnam, from Greene Tare, County Meath, Ireland; Pvt. John Dolan, from Killargua County, Ireland; Pvt. John Carey, from St. Joseph's Convent, Ayrshire, Scotland; Pvt. Thomas Shannon, from Cahersherkan, County Clare, Ireland; Pvt. Alexander Jornest, from Odessa, Russia; and 1st Lt. John Norman, from Seffle, Sweden. Lt. Norman's death was particularly memorable, in that he was among the first of the 165th's soldiers killed in action when a dugout in which he was sheltering with other solders was demolished by a German artillery bombardment on 7 March 1918. Poet and infantry Sgt. Joyce Kilmer would shortly thereafter write his famous work "Rouge Bouquet" to commemorate the deaths of his comrades.[3]

The New Yorkers of the 165th Infantry were not alone in having many foreign-born soldiers in their unit. The 151st Field Artillery, formed from Minnesota National

Pvt. Battista Targhetta was born in Italy in 1895. Included in the initial draft, Targhetta was assigned to the 158th Infantry Regiment, 40th Division, at Camp Kearny, California. In June 1918, the 40th became the 6th Depot Division, and Targhetta was transferred to the 9th Infantry Regiment, 2nd Division. With this hard-fighting unit Targhetta saw combat at St. Mihiel, Blanc Mont, and the Meuse-Argonne Offensive. *Courtesy New Mexico State Historical Service*

Guardsmen, reported that its ranks contained seven men born in Canada, four in Sweden, three in Austria, two each in England and Italy, and one each from Denmark, Switzerland, Norway, Germany, Ireland, and Poland.[4] In the Rainbow Division's 166th Infantry Regiment—an Ohio National Guard unit—the headquarters company alone reported it had soldiers from Intrebaegria and Sernoucalaza, Italy; Avastas, Sweden; and another from Galicia, Austria. The headquarters company of the 149th Field Artillery Regiment reported it had Canadians, Swedes, Russians, and even a native of Honolulu, Hawaii.[5] What makes these details from the 42nd Division all the more astounding is that they were compiled in October 1917, well before the effects of conscription would swell the manpower pool with foreign-born men ranging in age from eighteen to forty-five.

In late June, Pershing dispatched elements of his staff to search for appropriate training areas for the 1st Division and the follow-on units that were soon to arrive. When they returned, their recommendation was that the American training effort should be centered in the large area near Gondrecourt and Neufchâteau. These training sites would also support future operations in the Lorraine sector of the Western Front should that become the American sector.

Pershing also directed his staff to conduct an analysis of how best to organize the AEF for combat and logistical operations. The AEF would consist of thirty divisions

Chief Mechanic John Davis was born in Dublin, Ireland, in 1891. He enlisted in the Pennsylvania National Guard in November 1914, and was later assigned to the 107th Field Artillery Regiment when the 28th Division was formed. In France, Davis served in the Fisme-Vesle, Oise-Aisne, Meuse-Argonne, and Ypres-Lys Campaigns. He is seen here in the unit photograph taken in Le Mans, France, on 9 April 1919. *Courtesy Ryan Conroy*

divided into and controlled by five corps of six divisions each. In each corps would be corps-owned units, such as heavy artillery, long-range-signal, aviation, and observation balloon units, and engineer specialty units. In addition, one of the six divisions would be designated a depot division, and another would serve as the replacement division for making up combat losses of personnel in the four combat divisions. As these designs were being drawn up and discussed, more AEF units began to arrive in France, but at neither the speed nor efficiency the other Allies expected or hoped for.

The War Department was quickly finding out that, as hard as it was to build and train an expeditionary force, it was equally difficult to get them across the ocean to France. The rapid movement of troops from the camps to the eastern seaboard was greatly facilitated by railroads, but that efficiency sometimes made the problem worse. There simply were not enough ships to carry the Doughboys across the Atlantic Ocean. Aggravating the problem was the fact that, rather than assisting the Americans in getting the troops moving, the French and British insisted on setting their own priorities on what their transport ships would or could carry.

Struggling mightily to get the AEF moving toward the front, Gen. Tasker Bliss wrote in exasperation to Secretary Baker that the army had reached the point "where it is evident that if we do not send enough troops promptly, we must face the probability of losing the insufficient numbers that we may have sent."[6] Bliss had already established a centralized embarkation office and had commandeered the massive German-owned Hamburg American Lines port facilities in Hoboken, but even these actions were not enough.

Baker did what he could to help. After the April 1917 declaration of war, he authorized that German ships impounded in American ports be used as troop ships. This turned out to be more of

Born in San Giorgio, Italy, in 1896, Egidio Rinaldo was a shoemaker in New York City when the first draft took place. He was inducted at Fort Slocum in July 1917 and served in the 53rd Infantry Regiment, 6th Division, for the entire war. In this postwar, Paris-made portrait, he is wearing the six-pointed star patch of the 6th Division on his left shoulder.

Joaquin Bernardo Calvo de Leon was born at the Costa Rican Legation in Washington, DC, in 1893, son of the minister plenipotentiary of Costa Rica. He was working for an Ohio newspaper when he joined the US Army Ambulance Service in December 1917. He was credited with serving in the Somme Defensive, Montdidier-Noyon, Aisne, St. Mihiel, and Meuse-Argonne Campaigns and was awarded the French *Croix de Guerre* with Silver Star citation. *Courtesy Brian Grogan*

a challenge than expected due to the German captains and crews of captive ships. Fearing that their vessels would be used against their home country, they carried out a program of deliberate sabotage. Fortunately for the Americans, the Germans had not taken into consideration American skills with ship repair and electro-welding. Working around the clock and seven days a week, the repair crews brought the ships back to seaworthiness. By the time they were finished, the US Navy and shipyards had repaired and placed back into commission the German ships, most with new names and now flying the American flag.

With measles and pneumonia reaching epidemic levels at some camps, several congressmen announced that they would undertake an investigation of the war effort. Due to inadequate shelter and a shortage of heavy winter uniforms for sick soldiers, there were many complaints from the parents of soldiers undergoing training. The Army Medical Corps was also criticized for not properly segregating new soldiers from the general population until it could be determined whether or not they were carriers of infectious diseases.

In their defense, the medical staffs had tried to warn the army's leadership regarding the dangers of overcrowding troops into barracks and tents at training sites. And they certainly were not to blame for the uniform shortage. Unfortunately, the overwhelming need to train and field an army trumped all arguments and logic. That

Sharing a common surname and a common fate: Alexander Gorczynski (left) from Slyski, Poland, and John J. Gorczynski from Klon Komo, a Russian-controlled area of Poland. Alexander was a private 1st class in the 309th Infantry Regiment, 78th Division, when he was killed in action on 20 October 1918. His former commander wrote that "Gorczynski . . . was one of the most faithful and courageous men in the company." John Gorczynski was with the 310th Infantry Regiment, 78th Division, when he was killed in action on 23 September 1918. *Courtesy Rochester and Monroe County, NY*

said, with forty-one deaths from pneumonia at Camp Bowie, Texas, and sixty more at Camp Sevier, South Carolina, things could not get much worse for a secretary of war trying to move an army across a large country and a vast ocean to the battle line.

While awaiting the arrival of large numbers of units and soldiers from the States, AEF staff attempted to develop a meaningful training program that would ensure units would be combat ready when their turn came to go into the line. Their original plan was well thought out and was designed to slowly train the arriving units at the lowest individual maneuver level: the battalion. The training program called for a month of small-unit instruction at the battalion level, followed by another month at the battalion level in a relatively quiet trench sector. Thereafter, the battalions would rejoin their division for a month of large-scale unit training at regiment and then brigade level.[7]

While most of the arriving soldiers would be receiving standard unit-level training, a series of schools would be

Archelles Levesque, born in Quebec, Canada, was already a naturalized citizen living in Maine and operating a pool hall when he was drafted. Levesque, seen here in a French-made portrait, was originally assigned to the 303rd Infantry Regiment but was transferred to Base Hospital 208, which operated in the Autun area and then in Bordeaux. *Courtesy of Brennan C. Gauthier*

available to provide advanced and specialized instruction in leadership, artillery tactics, and general staff work. Unfortunately, the realities of the Western Front caused an almost immediate diversion of some units to French or British training sites upon arrival. The German 1918 spring offensives forced the AEF to further shorten and, in some cases, completely cancel the training planned for the newly arrived troops. As a result, "After April 1918 few divisions had a full four weeks in any [training] phase; for some the entire cycle was only a month."[8] It very quickly became a matter of plugging holes where needed. The best some newly arrived divisions could hope for was rudimentary training followed by service in a "quiet" defensive sector for some practical experience. This calculated risk also served to release the units currently in those sectors for duty in more-active areas.

One such new division was the 29th, which replaced the 32nd in the Alsace sector and was then in turn replaced by the 88th. It was not a great system, but the 29th had at least received some frontline combat experience (suffering 923 casualties, primarily from gas attacks) before being redeployed from Alsace to Verdun to serve in the

Meuse-Argonne Offensive. Other divisions arriving in late summer 1918 were not as lucky, and during the Meuse-Argonne campaign in October, their lack of tactical expertise showed.

Though most soldiers from the first draft were expected to have had at least six to eight months of training before arriving in France, that period was just the goal. While some had that and more, the greatest amount had less. The Source Records of the Great War reported:

> Seven months may then be taken as the average training figure for the first million men, five months for the second million. . . . After reaching France an average of two month's training before going into front-line trenches was maintained, although the experience of divisions used as replacements in the last months was under this figure.[9]

Replacement centers in France were kept busy providing ten days of remedial rifle skills training for soldiers who arrived in France.

As the first complete division in France, the 1st Division also received the first opportunity to show their mettle. Among the Doughboys of the 1st Engineer Regiment of the 1st Division was Polish-born Cpl. Boleslaw Suchocki. Like many immigrant soldiers, he struggled with the English language, yet his account, written in April 1919, of his experiences during the Battle of Cantigny (27–31 May 1918) makes for gripping reading. Suchocki, who was wounded prior to jump-off and refused evacuation, went over the top with the first wave, acting as a wire cutter for the following waves of infantrymen. He later described his approach to the wire:

> We passed the ruines and on the other side we find many orchorts [orchards] and also there was barbwire fence with four strings on wire about ten inches apart, it was hard to cross it, so I came to the post, knock the wires down with the but of my rifle, low enough to step over for us, and the others that were behind us, I jest moved on one side the post and a bullet struck the post and penetrated through that was another my good luck.

The WWI Victory Medal with bars for Meuse-Argonne and Defensive Sector, American Legion pin, and dog tags belonging to Cuban-born Jose V. Obregon. Born in Cienfuegos, Obregon was a clerk in a Packard automobile dealership in Boston prior to the war. *Courtesy Reynaldo Cervantes Jr.*

Suchocki, another engineer, and an infantryman carrying an automatic rifle approached a line of German trenches and dugouts:

First, the doughboy with the Automatic rifle was hurt in the right arm I and the other fellow ran to the trench, I saw that a Dutchman stick his head over the parapet I shot at him and he rolled in, into the trench. The doughboy was chasing another Dutchman but he did'nt shoot at him only was trying to stab him, the Dutchman grasp the doughboys bayonet with one hand and push it a side, bend the bayonet pretty bad right at the handle, I look at the struggle it was about ten feet a way from me, so I hollered shoot him but the Dutchman throw his hands up and hollered in German, "Don't shoot me I will tell you something." I said to the doughboy holt on, but it was too late, the shot fired and the Dutchman tumble down.

As Suchocki and the other men split up in the trenches, he came upon a dugout whose entrance was covered with a burlap curtain, and later wrote:

I saw that the cortain was moving I hollered few times "come rouse" but no one was coming out, so I open fire right at the hole, fired five rounds, then I hear of some kind of squiling [squealing] in the hole. I stepped closer to the trench and pull the top off, there was four men convulsively twisting in the trench. I turned around and saw that the doughboy was fighting with two men so I fired at one and he stabbed the other, but the Dutchman that were in the small holes saw it and start to come out by bunches three bullets penetrate my close [clothes], two below the waist and one in the right hand sleeve.

We laid down and start to shoot but that was only our good luck that the second wave reach the place and become boutchering [butchering], there rose over twenty Germans, throw their rifles down and stood with their arms up, the doughboys didn't pay attention only shoot at them and stab them too, one of the doughboys on the run stab a Dutchman that the bayonet went clear through.

At that point, Lt. Col. Robert J. Maxey, 28th Infantry Regiment, arrived on the scene to put a stop to the killing and get the men moving again. Suchocki was later awarded the Silver Star for his bravery during this battle.[10]

Although limited in size and scope compared to the battles that were coming, Cantigny was an important step in showing both the Allies and the enemy that the Doughboys had come to fight. Lawrence Stallings later wrote that the "Doughboys, in their first offensive action, had not only taken a position the Germans had never meant to lose, but had held it against three determined counterattacks."[11]

In counterpoint to Cpl. Suchocki was another incident just before the battle of Cantigny that also involved a foreign-born soldier. Just two weeks before the 1st Division was engaged in the Battle of Cantigny, the Germans captured Pvt. Yvan Nicoloff, a Bulgarian-born soldier in Company G, 26th Infantry Regiment. During interrogation, Nicoloff revealed the American forces in his area. He also told the Germans he knew of no prospects for an attack, but that the Americans were expecting a German attack. A German telegram sent to headquarters later that day stated:

Casualties in the company of this deserter slight. . . . Furloughs are denied. . . . In rear areas, with the exception of a few French in blue uniform only Chinese have been seen as labor troops. . . . Morale—indifferent. In the prisoner's company there are a few Turks, Austrians, and German-Americans who are waiting for an opportunity to desert. Reason of his desertion—his return to his home.

After the war, military authorities sought to prosecute Nicoloff, who had come back into American hands, for desertion. According to a letter written by division adjutant Lt. Col. Barnwell Legge on 13 July 1919:

It is believed that there are some soldiers in the 16th and 18th Infantry who, while prisoners of war saw Private Nicoloff, who it is alleged was in charge of American Prisoners of War in Germany.[12]

The letter further requested that officers check among the men to find out if there were others who were aware of the facts concerning Nicoloff. The final disposition of Nicoloff's case is unknown, but it shows that at least in some isolated instances enemy alien soldiers could indeed cause trouble.

Cantigny was followed on the calendar by battles at Chateau Thierry, at Belleau Wood, and along the Marne River. All of these involved AEF combat divisions as

the Allies struggled to contain the German summer offensives. Trained or not, the flood of Doughboys into France was now beginning to have an effect. Negotiations with the British over shipping priorities had been completed, and arrangements for American soldiers to be transported on their ships meant that daily almost 10,000 Doughboys were landing in France.

Pvt. First Class Giovanni (John) Rossi, a runner in Headquarters Company, 111th Infantry Regiment, 28th Division (back row, right), posing with friends after his discharge. Rossi, a native of Italy and an Italian army veteran, was drafted and assigned to the 159th Infantry Regiment, 40th Division, which became a depot division providing replacements to combat units; Rossi was one such man, sent to the 28th Division probably in August 1918. *Courtesy of Kurt Rossi*

By July 1918, the AEF was over a million strong and growing; this translated into twenty-three combat divisions, as well as the supporting logistical operation troops. More importantly, six of Pershing's divisions had received their baptism of fire and had held up well. Five more divisions were being trained in the British sector as part of the negotiated price for increased British shipping support.[13] Another six divisions were training in the area around Chaumont.

Four other US divisions were stationed with French units holding "quiet" sectors of the front in the Alsace region. Among the divisions in training behind the line was the 79th Division. Manned primarily with draftees from Baltimore, Philadelphia, the District of Columbia, and rural areas of Pennsylvania and Maryland, the division had trained at Camp Meade. The division had been harvested so many times to provide men for other units that few remained from the initial training group. By the time the 79th departed for France, their ranks reflected a very diverse membership. The 310th Field Artillery Regiment, equipped with 75 mm cannons, reported men from fifteen countries in their ranks, including Russia, Poland, Italy, Austria, Switzerland, England, Lithuania, Greece, and Germany.[14]

Pvt. Francesco (Frank) Stellato was born in Italy in 1890. He was drafted and reported for duty on 26 May 1918. A member of the 57th Pioneer Infantry Regiment, Stellato left the United States for France on 29 September. He probably came down with the flu while on board the *Leviathan*, since he died of "Broncho-pneumonia" on 9 October—very soon after his arrival—along with some 200 of his fellow 57th Pioneer Infantry soldiers. *Courtesy of Lou Ponsi*

Even the *Stars and Stripes*, published in Paris, France, noted the prevalence of foreign-born soldiers in the ranks. In a 28 February 1918 article, the newspaper reported that the US Army was "the most 'international' in history . . . [and wrote letters] in forty-six different languages. Out of 600 such letters . . . the chances are but half will be written in Italian followed in order of their numerousness by those inscribed in Polish, French and Scandinavian." The article further noted that the staff responsible for censoring soldier mail handled on a regular basis letters written in "twenty-five European languages, many tongues and dialects of the Balkan States and a scattering few in Yiddish, Chinese, Japanese, Hindu, Tahitian, Hawaiian, Persian and Greek, to say nothing of a number of Philippine dialects."[15]

As the pace of battle picked up in early autumn 1918, one of the problems remained the lack of time available for training newly inducted soldiers. One 37th Division Doughboy later noted that he had gone from draft notice to the front lines in 100 days.[16] It was the same in other units. Danish-born soldier Wilhelm Christian Andersen reported to Camp Cody in New Mexico after receiving his draft notice on 26 June 1918. Initially assigned to the 135th Infantry Regiment of the 34th Division, Andersen was transported by rail to Camp Dix, New Jersey, in August, and then across the Atlantic on ship to Britain in October. Just three days later he was in France. In a matter of four months, he had gone from being a draftee to serving in a combat zone. Although Andersen arrived too late to participate in combat operations, he did endure some of the hardships experienced by his earlier-arriving fellow soldiers. He wrote:

> Hiked to Forwarding Camp piched Tent out in the swamp that night in pouring down rain the next day November the 10th we went through the mill at La Mans [the mill was series of stations, including laundry and delousing, through which soldiers passed] and left for Clermont in the Argonne Forest arrived there Nov 12th.[17]

On arrival in the Verdun area the 34th Division was split up. Anderson was sent as a post-armistice replacement to Company F, 142nd Infantry Regiment, 36th Division, with which he served until his return to the United States and discharge in June 1919.

Even National Guard units, such as the 28th Division, which began the war with an almost entirely Pennsylvanian complement, struggled with the problem of receiving untrained soldiers as replacements. Their history recorded that due:

> to many replacements, some of whom were not the highest calibre, all of the Divisions had trouble from time to time to hold their lines when their men became nervous. With too brief training before leaving America, these replacements had been sent to combat divisions shortly after landing in France, and were as yet not totally assimilated. In the Twenty-eighth Division there were a number of Mexican half-breeds, who did not have the stamina or the understanding to remain cool under their first heavy fire and, had it not been for the courage and coolness of the main body of the men in the Division, and for the efficient backing up of the second line forces, more than one unit would doubtless have broken.[18]

The same narrative gave the example of the 110th Infantry Regiment, which started the war almost entirely made up of Pennsylvanians, but by mustering-out time, less than half the soldiers were from the "keystone state."[19] For better or worse, this mixing—at first done to hurriedly fill understrength units—had become intentional. US Army Chief of Staff Gen. Peyton March issued an order in August 1918, declaring, "This country has but one army. . . . Distinctive appellations, such as the Regular Army, Reserve Corps, National Guard, and National Army . . . will be discontinued."[20] As a result, the mixing of replacements from the different "armies," which had been done initially as an emergency measure, had now become actual Army policy. As to the problems previously mentioned, specifically regarding poorly trained foreign-born

Born in County Cork, Ireland, in 1891, Patrick Joseph Sullivan was assigned to the 308th Infantry Regiment, 77th Division. During a trench raid on 24 June 1918 by Germans on the American position near Baccarat, France, Sullivan was taken prisoner but refused to go with his captors. His body was found the next day with bayonet and rifle butt wounds. *Courtesy Rochester and Monroe County, NY*

soldiers, it must be added that the Meuse-Argonne was a tough classroom to learn soldier skills, and many units suffered from its harsh lessons.

In addition to the many divisions of Pershing's US First Army and the African American 93rd Division on loan to the French, there were two National Guard divisions (the 27th and 30th) that remained with the British Army and saw very heavy fighting in the Ypres-Lys Campaign, and in the Somme Offensive. Despite the many criticisms British and French Army leaders made about the Doughboys, their leaders, their training, and their performance in combat, none of the Allied leaders ever volunteered to relinquish control of the American units under their command.

Another and quite unexpected headache for the AEF headquarters staff was the large size of the US divisions. By their very size, the divisions were proving difficult to sustain in combat. It soon became obvious that the number of supply, maintenance, and transportation troops allocated to a division were insufficient to logistically support four infantry regiments, three artillery regiments, and an engineer regiment when they were fully engaged in combat operations.

One officer in the 3rd Division later described his unit's ration dump as just that, "a dump." Because of road congestion, the 3rd's quartermasters traveled as far forward as they could and left their cargo of bread and canned goods in a pile in a large hole near a collapsed dugout: "There was no system, no issue—anyone could carry away what he wanted."[21]

Cpl. Fiore Cosentino was born in Italy in 1892. An early draftee, Cosentino was assigned to Battery B, 304th Field Artillery Regiment, 77th Division. In November, he was sent to Motor Truck Company 307. Deploying overseas in January 1918, Cosentino served in various units, including the Motor Truck Division of the American Mission, Reserve Mallet, a US Army transportation unit supporting the French Army. *Courtesy of the Cosentino family*

Important for its clarity and its subject matter, this photograph shows Italian-born Anthony Anzevino and a comrade cooking bacon over a small fire pit made from chunks of concrete and barb wire. Despite the informal atmosphere of the picture, two important points are readily obvious: Anthony's gas mask is ready for immediate use and his rifle is spotlessly clean. Both are clear indications of a close proximity to the front lines and that these are well-disciplined troops. *Courtesy John Adams-Graf Collection*

If the supply system was a mess, the replacement system was little better. Many men who arrived in France in August were assigned as replacements and had to adapt to the front lines and trenches with minimal training. As replacements, they were forced to become part of a combat unit that had in many cases already been through the crucible of battle and had formed a cohesion based on that common ordeal. The new men had to fit into a group that would have been naturally wary of "outsiders"; perhaps the men who had difficulty with the English language suffered even more as they tried to blend in and assimilate into a close-knit group. The following case study illustrates this point.

For the 26 May 1918 draft, dozens of men from Kenosha, Wisconsin, were called up. The precise number of foreign-born men in this group is not known, but it must have been substantial. A random sample of fourteen of the foreign-born men in this draft reveals some striking similarities and also illustrates the difficult conditions that confronted these men and others, of whatever nativity, who were drafted during this time.

The origin of the men reflects the character of the Kenosha immigrant population of the time: nine from Italy, four from Russia, and one from England. All fourteen went through almost identical experiences. Reporting for duty in Kenosha on 26 May

1918, they were sent by train to the 161st Depot Brigade at Camp Grant. The 86th Division had been forming and training at Camp Grant since September 1917. As with other units, they had been raided for manpower since autumn 1917. They, in turn, had received draftees and transferees from other camps. After a few days of processing, the fourteen Kenosha men were transferred to the 337th Infantry Regiment, 85th Division, at Camp Custer, Michigan; at this time, 2,500 men were sent from the 86th to the 85th. The 85th Division, like the 86th Division, was trying to get sufficient manpower to go overseas.

In mid-July, the 85th Division left Camp Custer and headed for its port of embarkation and on 23 July 1918 sailed for Europe, arriving in mid-August. The 85th was then designated as the 4th Depot Division and began to provide replacements to combat units almost immediately. Between 15 and 25 August, thirteen of the Kenosha men were sent out as replacements; the fourteenth man was sent out on 8 October. Ten men went to the 1st Division, three went to the 3rd Division, and one (the man sent out on 8 October) went to the 35th Division. All the men sent out in August eventually saw combat.

The men who were assigned to the 1st Division (eight to the 26th Infantry Regiment and two to the 18th Infantry Regiment) were with their new unit only about two weeks before they were thrust into combat at St. Mihiel on 12 September. Of the

A group of US Doughboys, including a medical sergeant and an Asian soldier, pose for a group shot. The purpose of having the chicken in the photograph is unknown, but chances are very good he did not survive his encounter with the always-hungry Doughboys. *Courtesy of John Adams-Graf Collection*

ten men sent to the 1st Division, four were killed in action and four were wounded in action. All three of the men sent to the 3rd Division were in the 7th Infantry Regiment, and all three were wounded during the Meuse-Argonne Offensive. Of the thirteen foreign-born men in our sample, four were killed in action and seven were wounded in action, while only two men made it through unscathed.

From their initial reporting date (26 May) until the first men entered combat on 12 September was a span of only 109 days—not quite three and a half months. Considering that the men spent a week at Camp Grant for initial processing, equipment issue, and medical exams, they had less than two weeks available for training before their departure for Camp Custer. After arrival at Camp Custer, they spent at least another week in processing, allowing for less than a month for training prior to their departure for the port around 20 July. Take into account three weeks for sailing to England, traveling across England and into France, and then more processing before and after assignment as replacements, and one can readily see that the men must have had at most only a few weeks of effective training before assignment to a combat unit.

Admittedly this is a small sample size, but one can readily see that all men, foreign or native born, who were in such a situation faced a tough challenge. This small cross section does not allow us to determine whether language issues resulted in an increased likelihood of a man being killed or wounded, but if one factors in a possible language handicap (except for the man born in England), one can appreciate the situation that confronted the men.

| Name | Country | Unit | KIA/WIA |
|---|---|---|---|
| Michael Bruno | Italy | 139th Inf Rgt | None |
| Antonio Cerminara | Italy | 26th Inf Rgt | None |
| Carmine Chiappetta | Italy | 18th Inf Rgt | WIA Sep 12 |
| Louis Chiappetta | Italy | 7th Inf Rgt | WIA Oct 21 |
| Benjamin Conforti | Italy | 7th Inf Rgt | WIA Oct 12 |
| Joe Covelli | Italy | 18th Inf Rgt | WIA Oct 5 |
| Ernest Davey | England | 26th Inf Rgt | None |
| Charles Gechas | Russia | 26th Inf Rgt | KIA Oct 5 |
| John Lonika | Russia | 26th Inf Rgt | KIA Oct 1-11 |
| Joseph Lukowski | Russia | 26th Inf Rgt | KIA Oct 2 |
| Mike Milazewski | Russia | 26th Inf Rgt | WIA Sep 12 |
| Frank Muto | Italy | 26th Inf Rgt | WIA Oct 5 |
| Emilio Petrocchi | Italy | 26th Inf Rgt | KIA Sep 12 |
| Peter Scola | Italy | 7th Inf Rgt | WIA Oct 5 |

Examining the history of one of these men serves to illustrate the struggle and drama associated with their service. Carmine Chiappetta was born in Italy and came to the United States in 1903, working for nine years before returning to Italy to get married and start a family. Chiappetta was living in the United States when war was declared, and he registered for the draft in June 1917. Chiappetta ended up with Company G, 18th Infantry Regiment, 1st Division, on 26 August 1918, just in time to receive hurried training and attempt assimilation into his company prior to the St. Mihiel Offensive, slated to begin on 12 September.[22]

The 1st Division was to be a key part of the initial assault; the immediate objective was to reduce the St. Mihiel salient dominated by Mont Sec, a large prominence that had allowed the German army a clear view of allied lines. The 18th Infantry Regiment was to drive forward and then conduct a flanking movement to the west to guard against attack from Mont Sec.

After marching in the driving rain and then witnessing a tremendous US artillery bombardment, the men jumped off at 5:30 a.m. Advancing through mud, the men at times climbed over barbed-wire belts rather than use wire cutters. Although casualties were relatively light, men were struck down.

At about 7:30 a.m., Chiappetta went down with a serious gunshot wound to the head. According to a doctor, years later he had "a very hazy memory of his wound." He told the doctor that he remembered "going over the top and also digging a hole to get into and awoke in hospital. Says he never saw any of his Company again." He also suffered a leg wound at the same time. Probably some members of Company G saw Chiappetta shot in the head, or perhaps stretcher bearers who picked him up later saw the severity of his wounds. In any event, he was initially reported as killed in action, but he was very much alive when he was brought into Field Hospital Number 3, where he was given morphine, hot drinks, and hot water. He was then evacuated to Mobile Hospital Number 39.

There doctors recorded the following: "Wound 7:30 AM Sept 12/18 by shrapnel. . . . Penetrating wound upper 1/3 R. thigh outer no exit R. foot very cold . . . no plantar upper. Wound of skull, spattering

Wilhelm Christian Anderson, a native of Copenhagen, Denmark, was thirty years old when he was drafted. After a very short training period, Anderson was sent to France and was assigned to the 36th Division just after the armistice. Somewhat unexpectedly, Anderson is equipped with a 1917 Enfield rifle; he served in National Guard units and should have been equipped with a 1903 model Springfield. *Courtesy New Mexico Commission of Public Records*

A truly unique photograph, unfortunately from an unidentified unit, that gives the country of origin of each soldier instead of their names. The key to the numbered helmets are 1. Poland; 2. Philippines; 3. Mexico; 4. Germany; 5. Ecuador; 6. Turkey; 7. Alsace Lorraine; 8. Greece; and 9. Austria. What is equally interesting is that at least four and maybe five (Alsace Lorraine) could be considered enemy countries or territories.

The service abstract card for Duggu Ramn, born in the city Simula Hill, in the eastern portion of India. Ramn was assigned to the 304th Engineers, 79th Division, and was wounded in a gas attack during the Meuse-Argonne Offensive. After the war Ramn received $200 from the Pennsylvania Veterans compensation and is buried in the Philadelphia National Cemetery. *Courtesy Pennsylvania Archives, Ancestry.com®*

in area of wound. No depression of cranium observed . . . thigh right no T.B or fracture observed."[23]

From the hospital, Chiappetta was sent to Base Hospital Number 22, where he was diagnosed with "Comp. Fr. left parietal bone, 1 cm. left med. line." Apparently a machine gun bullet struck the top left part of his skull a glancing blow and broke his skull without penetrating the skin. The size of the wound would variously be described as one inch square, one centimeter square, etc. A physician's report dated January 1919 stated: "Hit by machine gun bullet, destruction of bone about 1 inch in diameter on or about coronal section left side of skull. Scar extending deeply and

The soldiers of Company F, 109th Infantry, 28th Division, pose during the winter of 1918–1919. The soldier on the right in the first row has been tentatively identified as Puerto Rican–born Jose Olivera. Of note here is the mixture of Enfield and Springfield rifles; Army policy of the period was that the National Guard and Regular Army units would be issued Springfields and the National Army would receive Enfields. *Courtesy Pennsylvania, WWI Veterans Service and Compensation Files, 1917–1919*

depressed." Chiappetta next made his way through various hospitals on his way home while still being listed as killed in action, and a telegram sent to his wife notified her of her husband's "death."[24]

Another doctor wrote: "There is a period of complete amnesia from time of injury until he reached Base Hospital #22, 15 days later. He was unable to talk until December, 1918 when his power of speech slowly returned." Chiappetta left France aboard the *Pochahontas* on 7 November. In the States he went to various hospitals until his discharge on January 5, 1919. At one of the hospitals in France he was finally recognized by someone who knew him, and his family received word that he was still alive.

Chiappetta was almost certainly discharged before he was medically ready to reenter civilian life. For the next few years he was in and out of hospitals seeking treatment for his wound and various complications associated with it, including depression. As one doctor concluded:

An unidentified but well-equipped Asian Doughboy poses for a portrait with his field gear and fur-lined mittens in a makeshift French photo studio. *Courtesy John Adams-Graf Collection*

[Chiappetta] received a gun shot wound of the skull which did not enter but ricocheting caused a compound depressed fracture in the left parietal region, nearly circular, two inches in diameter. The base of the skull was removed at the time and now nothing covers the Dura but the hairless scalp. The skin of this area is very unhealthy and is not completely healed. It seems strange that he should have been discharged without complete recovery.[25]

Despite health issues associated with his severe wounds, Chiappetta continued to work and provide for his family until his death in 1955.

Some of the men who served in the 85th Division/4th Depot Division without being sent out as replacements got their chance to occupy an active sector. Vincent Presta was born in Italy and was living in Kenosha, Wisconsin, when he was drafted. He reported for duty in September 1917 and was then sent to Camp Custer as part of the 340th Infantry Regiment, 85th Division. Presta "saw war service for the United States as a chance, an opportunity and a moral duty, to further the cause of 'good' in

Tom Saydes, a 362nd Infantry Regiment, 91st Division soldier and immigrant from Sayditsa, Greece. Saydes, a resident of Midvale, Utah, was inducted into the US Army in April 1918, and was wounded in the Meuse-Argonne Campaign just five months later. *Courtesy of Brennan C. Gauthier*

Serving with the 1st Division in France and later in the occupation of Germany was Norwegian-born Otto Emil Holmdahl. Here Holmdahl, a gardener in civilian life, poses in the well-known Theodor Loos Photography Studio at Number 2 *Schloss Strasse* in Coblenz, Germany.

the world and stop the 'bad guys' from doing any more bad."[26] A clarinet player, Presta sought duty with the regimental band, figuring he would have a better chance of surviving the war as a musician than as an infantryman. As part of the 340th Regimental Headquarters Company, Presta sailed for France. He was not one of the men sent forward as a replacement, but stayed with the regiment as it trained incoming men for duty at the front. In October 1918, the 85th Division was assigned to the new American Second Army as a regional replacement division. For this service the 340th Infantry Regiment received credit for manning a defensive sector for the last two days of the war.

Mike Michalek, a native of Grodiro, Russia, was born in 1892, and worked in the steel mills in Pittsburgh until he was inducted into the Army. He first served at Camp Lee then deployed to France with the 45th Engineer Battalion, a railway maintenance unit. *Courtesy Brennan C. Gauthier*

Presta returned home and was discharged in early April 1919. He later tersely summed up his experiences: "War is bad."[27]

It is appropriate to examine some brief histories of other foreign-born soldiers in the AEF; these examples are in some ways typical, but in other ways they are exceptional. Among the many soldiers, there were several who lied about their age to enlist. This group included Salvatore Rucchetto and Carmine Belmonte, both Italian immigrants who enlisted at the age of seventeen. Rucchetto's service is discussed elsewhere; Belmonte enlisted in the US Army Air Service in January 1918, one month before his eighteenth birthday.

Assigned to the 1st Construction Company, Belmonte was sent to Chattis Hill, Hampshire, England, to help construct an airfield for American squadrons that were to fly the Handley-Page aircraft. The 1st Construction Company spent the war in England working on various construction projects for the Air Service.[28]

Older men served too. Some "old soldier" immigrants achieved comparatively high rank in the military. Mostly they were men who had come to America in the late nineteenth century and joined the military soon thereafter.

George A. Campbell was born on Prince Edward Island, Canada, in 1869. Campbell joined the US Army in 1889. As a Regular Army soldier he saw active service against the Indians in the American West and later in Cuba, the Philippines, and China, and along the Mexican border. When America entered World War I, Campbell applied for a commission and was eventually offered a captaincy. As the commander of Company E, 18th Infantry Regiment, 1st Division, he was killed in action on 4 October 1918 during the Meuse-Argonne Offensive, while leading his company in the attack on Hill 240. Campbell received the Distinguished Service Cross and the French *Croix de Guerre* for his bravery in action.[29]

Hjalmar Erickson was born in Tonsberg, Norway, and came to the United States in 1889. He enlisted in the Army as a private in the 8th Cavalry Regiment and was commissioned a second lieutenant in 1899. By 1918, he was a colonel commanding the 26th Infantry Regiment, 1st Division. According to Lt. Col. Theodore Roosevelt Jr., who succeeded Erickson in command of the 26th, he "was a fine troop leader and a powerful man physically." He also possessed an intense belief in caring for his troops. When his regiment was engaged in dire combat in the Meuse-Argonne Offensive and the officer in charge of ensuring that food was brought up for the troops during the night failed in his duty, Erickson called a meeting of battalion commanders and the officer in charge of rations. Maj. Lyman S. Frasier, commanding the 3rd Battalion, described what happened:

> After considerable heated telephone conversation the three battalion commanders and the officer detailed to see that food reached the forward troops were assembled in conference with the regimental commander [Erickson]. A dramatic and tense moment took place. The regimental commander spoke somewhat broken English. He said, in effect, "Dere is von officer here vot is a ----------. He vill at vonce get himself out of my P.C." Needless to say the officer concerned with rations left and did not stop going until he was safe within the continental limits of the United States.[30]

Pvt. Carmine Chiappetta, Company G, 18th Infantry Regiment, 1st Division (on right) and brother Pasquale. Carmine was seriously wounded at St. Mihiel on 12 September 1918. *Courtesy of Christine Chiappetta Thorsen*

An unusual portrait captured inside a heart shows Italian-born Giovanni Morone of the 320th Infantry Regiment, 80th Division. Morone, a veteran of St. Mihiel and the Meuse-Argonne Offensives, has chosen to pose while wearing his woolen shirt with collar disks, an Honorable Discharge pin in his left-pocket buttonhole, and a nice fountain pen in his right pocket.

Polish-born Cpl. Anthony Hilbruner poses and shows off his corporal stripes, two overseas stripes, his *fouregerre* earned from his service in Company I, 18th Infantry Regiment, 1st Division, and an unauthorized set of officer's leather leggings. *Courtesy 1st Division Museum at Cantigny*

Lt. Col. John A. Paegelow, a native of Berlin, Germany, served as the balloon observation unit officer for the US First Army. In this capacity he had responsibility for all the assigned balloon units. At one point on 10 August 1918, US balloons in one area had to be hauled down due to the haze obscuring the front line. When German artillery began to shell US artillery positions, Paegelow hurried out to one of the balloon companies to see about the lack of a US response. Paegelow soon found Lt. Allan McFarland, commander of the balloon company, who later reported, "[Paegelow] roared in his thick German accent, 'Gott tam it Mac—vat for iss da palloon? I'm getting Hell from Corps!'" McFarland got the message and soon had his men prepare and raise a balloon.[31]

The rapid growth of the National Guard divisions had stretched the number of available officers to the limit, especially those trained in the intricacies of good staff work. As a result, some Regular Army sergeants found themselves promoted to officers and assigned to National Guard units.

Maj. John Cutchins, serving on the staff of the 29th Division, recounted an episode in which a German-born NCO—now a lieutenant—from the Regular Army expressed his amazement at an attack being carried out by Doughboys of the 29th. The "Old Army" former sergeant said, "Mein Gott, Major, chust tink of it: dere are men leading companies today what don't know how to make out a morning report." The former sergeant's close resemblance to a famous German general was also noted by many, and even 29th Division Commander Maj. Gen. Charles Morton referred to him as "Hindenburg."[32]

American Army nurses were among the first soldiers sent to France after the United States' declaration of war, and depending on which hospital they were assigned they ran the risk of hostile fire.

Born in 1889 in Trondheim, Norway, Lorentz Julius Kjelvik (third from left, back row) poses with the other members of his company, an interesting combination of Scandinavian and Native American draftees. Kjelvik served in Company C of the 340th Machine Gun Battalion, 89th Division. *Courtesy BG Marshall Kjelvik*

Reserve Nurse Beatrice Mary Mac-Donald, a native of Prince Edward Island, Canada, went overseas in May 1917. She was working with the surgical team at British Casualty Clearing Station 61 on 17 August 1917, when that unit came under aerial attack. MacDonald "continued at her post of duty caring for the sick and wounded until [she] was seriously wounded by a German bomb, thereby losing one eye." After recovery, she continued to serve in France until her discharge in April 1919. MacDonald earned the Distinguished Service Cross for heroism during the German air raid; she also earned the Distinguished Service Medal, the British Military Medal, and the French *Croix de Guerre*.[33]

Despite the many difficulties faced in France, particularly during the Meuse-Argonne Offensive, native-born and foreign-born Doughboys seemed determined to make the best of the situation. Perhaps they drew some comfort from the knowledge that behind them, in the States, was a continually growing military force that would soon be available to join them in the fight. It may also have been a comfort to know that the United States was truly a "nation at war" and that most citizens, even on the home front, appeared willing to do their part. Before we turn to that home front for insight into their war and efforts, it is important to take a closer look at some of the interesting individuals who were part of the great military force the United States was sending to France.

Anna Marie (Annie) Williams was born in Northamptonshire, England, in December 1885. She graduated from the Training School for Nurses at Erie County Hospital in Buffalo, New York, and deployed to France as part of Base Hospital Number 19. She contracted a very virulent and deadly form of the flu in October 1918, and died in Vichy, France, where she was buried before being disinterred and returned to the States. *Courtesy Rochester and Monroe County, NY*

The Zukajatics (also Zuhajtys) brothers, Frank and Mike, were originally from Sobolik, Poland, and were Russian citizens until they were naturalized. Frank served in the 29th Field Artillery Regiment, 5th Division, and Mike was wounded twice while serving with the 47th Infantry Regiment, 4th Division. *Courtesy Genesee County, Michigan, Archives*

The model M1917 Service Coat belonging to Pvt. Peter K. Droukas. Droukas, born in Sparta, Greece, immigrated to the United States in 1906. After training at Camp Devens, Massachusetts, Droukas deployed to France and was assigned to the 4th Division. He saw service in the front lines in the Second Battle of the Marne, at Chateau-Thierry, and at the Vesle River, where he was severely gassed in August 1918. *Courtesy Rogier van de Hoef*

This unusual and personalized gas mask carrier includes a full-length caricature of screen star Charlie Chaplain and the family crest and signature for "Fuligni." The artist was Benedetto Fuligni, an Italian-born soldier who served in the 303rd Infantry Regiment, 76th Division. *Courtesy of AdvanceGuardMilitaria.com*

## CHAPTER SIX

# BIOGRAPHIES

The [third battalion, 116th Infantry Regiment] received 340 untrained men, ten per cent of whom could speak no English, and many others but a few words. These men had been shunted back and forth across 4 different army camps. They were, however, patriotic Americans, willing and eager to serve their country.[1]

While selecting biographies for inclusion in this chapter, it quickly became apparent that the hardest task would be to limit the number. The AEF and the stateside Army were filled with many notable characters and interesting individuals. What follows is our attempt to provide information on a few of the Doughboys from foreign lands who left their unique mark on US military history.

### Jake Allex (13 July 1887–28 August 1959)

Cpl. Allex was born in Prizren, Serbia, in 1887. He was assigned to the 131st Infantry Regiment of the 33rd Division, a unit composed primarily of Illinois National Guardsmen. Allex was awarded the Medal of Honor for his actions at Chipilly Ridge, France, on 9 August 1918.

His Medal of Honor citation reads:

> At a critical point in the action, when all the officers with his platoon had become casualties, Cpl. Allex took command of the platoon and led it forward until the advance was stopped by fire from a machinegun nest. He then advanced alone for about 30 yards in the face of intense fire and attacked the nest. With his bayonet he killed 5 of the enemy, and when it was broken, used the butt of his rifle, capturing 15 prisoners.[2]

Allex ended the war as a sergeant. He died 28 August 1959, in a Veterans Administration hospital in Chicago. He is buried in the Serbian Orthodox Monastery of Saint Sava cemetery in Libertyville, Illinois.

## Johannes Siegfried Anderson (30 July 1887–15 April 1950)

First Sgt. Anderson was born in Finland. He was assigned to the 132nd Infantry Regiment, 33rd Division. Anderson was awarded the Medal of Honor for his actions at Consenvoye, France, on 8 October 1918. His Medal of Honor citation reads:

> While his company was being held up by intense artillery and machinegun fire, 1st Sgt. Anderson, without aid, voluntarily left the company and worked his way to the rear of the nest that was offering the most stubborn resistance. His advance was made through an open area and under constant hostile fire, but the mission was successfully accomplished, and he not only silenced the gun and captured it, but also brought back with him 23 prisoners.[3]

Anderson is buried in Acacia Park Cemetery and Mausoleum in Chicago, Illinois.

## Irving Berlin (11 May 1888–22 September 1989)

Born in Russia as Israel Isidore Baline, Irving Berlin was a well-known composer and lyricist before he was drafted into the US Army. His most famous work to that point was "Alexander's Ragtime Band," which became known internationally and is credited with starting a dance craze. After induction, he was stationed at Camp Upton on Long Island with the 152nd Depot Brigade. While there, Berlin put his considerable talents to work and wrote a musical about Army training. After the war his career became even more notable, as he was soon considered to be one of the great songwriters of the period. With his incredible longevity and his feel for what kind of music America wanted to hear, his successes were numerous. Among his most famous songs are "Easter Parade," "White Christmas," "There's No Business Like Show Business," "Anything You Can Do, I Can Do Better," and "Blue Skies." Perhaps his most famous song, "God Bless America," was written while he was in the Army, although it would not be performed for another twenty years. Berlin even found time to write another military-themed screenplay during World War II called "This Is the Army." He died in 1989 at age 101.[4]

The adjutant general's office Form 724 for Irving Berlin. It is interesting to note that he was demoted from sergeant to private on 21 October 1918, only to be promoted back to sergeant just four days later. Berlin would write some of his best-known songs, including "God Bless America," while at Camp Upton. *Courtesy New York, Abstracts of Military Service, 1917–1919*

**Raymond Buma (15 November 1896–27 September 1918)**

Cpl. Buma was born in Ijlst, Friesland, Holland, and later moved to Massachusetts, where he found work as a machinist. He enlisted in the US Army on 1 January 1918 at Fort Slocum, New York. He was assigned to the Machine Gun Company of the 39th Infantry Regiment, 4th Division, and deployed with the division to France in May 1918. Promoted to corporal by September, Buma earned the Distinguished Service Cross later that month. Unfortunately, the medal had to be awarded posthumously, since Cpl. Buma was killed in action the day after his heroic act. Buma is buried in Pine Grove Cemetery, Northbridge, Worcester County, Massachusetts.[5]

**Louis Cukela (1 May 1888–19 March 1956)**

Sgt. Louis Cukela was born in Sebenes, Austria (now Sibenik, Croatia), and enlisted in the US Army in 1914, serving until 1916. On 31 January 1917, he enlisted in the Marine Corps. He was assigned to the 66th Company of the 5th Regiment of Marines in the 2nd Division and served with the regiment throughout all its campaigns. Cukela was awarded both the Army and the Navy versions of the Medal of Honor for his actions near Villers-Cotterets, France, on 18 July 1918. His Navy Citation reads:

> For extraordinary heroism while serving with the 66th Company, 5th Regiment, during action in the Forest de Retz, near Viller-Cottertes, France, 18 July 1918. Sgt. Cukela advanced alone against an enemy strong point that was holding up his line. Disregarding the warnings of his comrades, he crawled out from the flank in the face of heavy fire and worked his way to the rear of the enemy position. Rushing a machinegun emplacement, he killed or drove off the crew with his bayonet, bombed out the remaining part of the strong point with German hand grenades and captured 2 machineguns and 4 men.[6]

Cukela continued his Marine Corps career after the war and rose to the rank of major while serving in varied duty assignments around the world. He also served during the occupation of the German Rhineland as part of the US Third Army's Rhine River Patrol.[7] Combining his US Army and Marine service, Cukela had almost thirty-two years of active duty when he retired.

Born in Austrian-ruled Croatia, Louis Cukela immigrated to the United States and joined the Army in 1914. He later enlisted in the Marine Corps and, while assigned to the 5th Regiment of Marines, was awarded both the Army and Navy versions of the Medal of Honor for his bravery in combat in July 1918. *Courtesy USMC HD*

**George Dilboy (5 February 1896–18 July 1918)**

Dilboy was born in Ottoman, Turkey, near the city of Izmir, in a Greek settlement called Alatsata. Growing up as a Greek in this region meant that Dilboy's youth was spent in a very dangerous and violent part of the world. Seeking a better and more peaceful life, George's father immigrated to Somerville, Massachusetts, in 1908.

In 1910, George joined him in America but returned to Greece just two years later to serve in the Greek army. He fought in the First Balkan War in 1912, and again the following year in the Second Balkan War. Dilboy returned to Massachusetts shortly thereafter and volunteered to serve in the National Guard in the Mexican border campaign. With the US entry into the war, Dilboy soon found himself back in Europe as a member of Company H, 103rd Infantry Regiment, 26th "Yankee" Division. During heavy fighting in late July, Dilboy proved his personal courage by attacking a German machine gun nest in Belleau, France, on 18 July 1918.[8] His Medal of Honor citation reads:

> After his platoon had gained its objective along a railroad embankment, Pfc. Dilboy, accompanying his platoon leader to reconnoiter the ground beyond, was suddenly fired upon by an enemy machinegun from 100 yards. From a standing position on the railroad track, fully exposed to view, he opened fire at once, but failing to silence the gun, rushed forward with his bayonet fixed, through a wheat field toward the gun emplacement, falling within 25 yards of the gun with his right leg nearly severed above the knee and with several bullet holes in his body. With undaunted courage he continued to fire into the emplacement from a prone position, killing 2 of the enemy and dispersing the rest of the crew.[9]

The desecration of Medal of Honor recipient George Dilboy's original grave in his hometown of Alatsata by Turkish soldiers so angered US President Warren Harding that he dispatched a Navy ship to recover the remains. Dilboy is now buried in Arlington National Cemetery.

Dilboy's medal was presented posthumously because he died of his wounds shortly after the battle. George's father requested that his remains be buried at his birthplace in Alatsata. This was done in a large ceremony witnessed by thousands of mourners and onlookers. During the 1919–1922 Greco-Turkish War, Turkish soldiers seized the town and vandalized the church and cemetery where the American hero was buried. Dilboy's coffin was broken into and his remains were scattered throughout the graveyard. Upon learning of this, President Warren G. Harding dispatched the USS *Litchfield* to Turkey to recover

Dilboy's remains and return them to the United States. George Dilboy was reburied in Arlington National Cemetery on 12 November 1923.

**Father Francis Patrick Duffy (2 May 1871–26 June 1932)**
Francis Duffy was born in Cobourg, Ontario, Canada, and studied at St. Michael's College in Toronto. He entered St. Francis Xavier's College in New York City as a teacher while continuing his studies. Duffy received a master of arts degree and was ordained a Catholic priest on 6 September 1896. St. Mary's Seminary, Baltimore, honored him with a doctor of divinity degree in 1904. He received several other high-level theological degrees, but none of these seemed as important to him as the men of the 165th Infantry Regiment to whom he ministered. He was known to all the men of the Rainbow Division simply as "Father." In their divisional history *Americans All, the Rainbow at War* the historians wrote:

> Father Duffy was as American as it is possible for any man to be, yet all the blood that flowed through his veins was Irish blood. This probably accounts for a compelling attraction the Army had for him. Because of the infernal character of war, Father Duffy did not admire it—but he loved the work of saving the souls of men engaged in war. When America entered the World War, along with HIS

Long after Father Duffy had packed away his uniforms and returned to being a civilian priest, he continued to tend to "his boys." Fiorello LaGuardia, mayor of New York City and a former Doughboy aviator, paid tribute to the priest at the 1937 dedication ceremony for the Father Duffy statue in Duffy Square, near Times Square and Broadway in New York City. *Courtesy NYDMNA*

BOYS of the old FIGHTING SIXTY-NINTH, Father Duffy went to face every peril that they were to be called upon to face. He was beloved by the men of his own Regiment, and of all other Regiments of the Division . . .[10]

After the war, Father Duffy remained dedicated to helping the men of his former unit while serving as the chaplain of the National Association of the Rainbow Division. Ironically, it was the very makeup of the 42nd division, coming from National Guard units of twenty-six states and the District of Columbia, that made their association truly a national one. Father Duffy passed away in 1932 after suffering from colitis.

### Matej Kocak (3 December 1882–4 October 1918)

Sgt. Kocak was born in Gbely (Slovakia), Austria, in 1882. He immigrated to the United States in 1906 and enlisted in the Marine Corps the following year. During his second enlistment he served in the Verz Cruz expedition. He was serving with the 66th Company of the 5th Regiment of Marines in the 2nd Division when he was awarded both the Army and Navy versions of the Medal of Honor for his actions near Soissons, France, on 18 July 1918. His Navy Medal of Honor citation reads:

> For extraordinary heroism while serving with the Sixty-Sixth Company, Fifth Regiment, Second Division, in action in the Viller-Cottertes section, south of Soissons, France, 18 July 1918. When a hidden machine gun nest halted the advance of his battalion, Sergeant Kocak went forward alone unprotected by covering fire and worked his way in between the German positions in the face of heavy enemy fire. Rushing the enemy position with his bayonet, he drove off the crew. Later the same day, Sergeant Kocak organized French colonial soldiers who had become separated from their company and led them in attacking another machine gun nest, which was also put out of action.[11]

Kocak was killed in action a few months later at Blanc Mont.[12]

### Walter Krueger (26 January 1881–20 August 1967)

Krueger was born in Flatow, West Prussia (known today as Złotów, Poland), to Julius (a Franco-Prussian War veteran) and Anna Krüger. When Julius died, Anna moved the family to St. Louis, Missouri. In 1898, Krueger enlisted in the Army to serve in the Spanish-American War. He reenlisted to serve in the Philippines and was promoted to sergeant.

Krueger was later commissioned an officer in the 30th Infantry Regiment. He served in the 26th and 84th Divisions during the First World War and by October 1918 was the chief of staff for the Army's growing Tank Corps. During the occupation of Germany, Krueger served as assistant chief of staff for IV Corps. On returning to the States, he attended command and staff courses, served again in the Philippines, and then became a language instructor at Leavenworth because of his fluency in Spanish, German, and French.

In May 1941, as Lt. Gen. Krueger, he took command of the Third Army, the same organization in which he served in 1919. In January 1943, Krueger assumed command of the Sixth Army based in Australia and guided it throughout campaigns in New Britain, New Guinea, Leyte, Mindoro, and Luzon. He was also credited with forming the special operations and reconnaissance force known as the Alamo Scouts. Promoted to general in March 1945, Krueger commanded the Sixth Army during the Occupation of Japan. Krueger retired in 1946, as the first soldier ever to rise through the ranks from private to four-star general.[13]

### Berger Holton Loman (24 August 1886–9 May 1968)

Pvt. Loman was born in Bergen, Norway, and served in Company H, 132nd Infantry Regiment, 33rd Division. He was awarded the Medal of Honor for his actions near Consenvoye, France, on 9 October 1918. His Medal of Honor citation reads:

> When his company had reached a point within 100 yards of its objective, to which it was advancing under terrific machinegun fire, Pvt. Loman voluntarily and unaided made his way forward after all others had taken shelter from the direct fire of an enemy machinegun. He crawled to a flank position of the gun and, after killing or capturing the entire crew, turned the machinegun on the retreating enemy.[14]

Loman lived to be eighty-one years old and is buried in Arlington National Cemetery.

### James I. Mestrovitch (May 22 1894–4 November 1918)

Sgt. Mestrovitch was born in Montenegro and immigrated to the United States in 1913. He served in the 111th Infantry Regiment of the 28th Division, a unit comprising mainly Pennsylvania National Guardsmen. He was awarded the Medal of Honor for his actions at Fismette, France, on 10 August 1918. His Medal of Honor citation reads:

> Seeing his company commander lying wounded 30 yards in front of the line after his company had withdrawn to a sheltered position behind a stone wall, Sgt. Mestrovitch voluntarily left cover and crawled through heavy machinegun and shell fire to where the officer lay. He took the officer upon his back and crawled to a place of safety, where he administered first-aid treatment, his exceptional heroism saving the officer's life.[15]

Mestrovitch died from Spanish flu one week before the armistice was signed. During the 1920s, his remains were carried by a US Navy vessel from France to Montenegro, and he was buried in the cemetery of his home village's Serbian Orthodox Church of St. John.

### Wladyslaw Tabara (2 March 1893–1978)

Tabara was born in Jlow, in what is now Poland, some sixty miles from Warsaw; he immigrated to the United States in 1912. He was working as a "finisher" for Joseph Fahys & Company, a well-known watchmaker in Sag Harbor, New York, when he was inducted into the Army. While serving with Company M, 308th Infantry Regiment, 77th Division, Pvt. Tabara participated in the Oise-Aisne Offensive. He was awarded the Distinguished Service Cross for his personal bravery in September 1918.[16]

**Antonio J. Tavano, (21 August 1891–unknown)**
Sgt. Tavano was born in Gimigliano, Italy, and was living in Union, New Jersey, when he registered for the draft. He was assigned to the 111th Machine Gun Battalion, 57th Infantry Brigade, 29th Division, a National Guard unit originally composed of soldiers from the 2nd and 3rd New Jersey Infantry Regiment's machine gun companies. By the time the 29th Division was sent into the Meuse-Argonne Offensive, Tavano was a member of Company D and had been promoted to sergeant. On 11 October 1918, Tavano exhibited great personal bravery and was awarded the Distinguished Service Cross.[17]

**Joseph "Colonel Joe" Henry Thompson (26 September 1871–1 February 1928)**
Thompson immigrated to the United States from the town of Kilkeel, in County Down, Ireland, in 1898, at age eighteen, and entered Geneva College in upstate New York. He was a star athlete in basketball, wrestling, and gymnastics at Geneva. He subsequently joined the Geneva football team and served as their player coach for three years. Thompson then continued his education at the University of Pittsburgh and also starred on their football team, leading them to a perfect season in 1904. Thompson graduated from Pitt in 1905 then went on to earn a law degree. As a major, Thompson served in the 110th Infantry Regiment of the 28th Division, comprising primarily Pennsylvania National Guardsmen. He was awarded the Medal of Honor for his actions near Apremont, France, on 1 October 1918. His Medal of Honor citation reads:

Counterattacked by 2 regiments of the enemy, Maj. Thompson encouraged his battalion in the front line of constantly braving the hazardous fire of machineguns and artillery. His courage was mainly responsible for the heavy repulse of the enemy. Later in the action, when the advance of his assaulting companies was held up by fire from a hostile machinegun nest and all but 1 of the 6 assaulting tanks were disabled, Major Thompson, with great gallantry and coolness, rushed forward on foot 3 separate times in advance of the assaulting line, under heavy machinegun and antitank-gun fire, and led the 1 remaining tank to within a few yards of the enemy machinegun nest, which succeeded in reducing it, thereby making it possible for the infantry to advance.[18]

After the war he practiced law in Beaver Falls, Pennsylvania, until his untimely death in 1928, as a result of ailments aggravated by his old war wounds.

**Michael Valente (5 February 1895–10 January 1976)**
Pvt. Michael Valente was born in Cassino, Italy, a place that would have great significance in the Second World War. He was assigned to the 107th Infantry Regiment in the 27th Division, a unit composed primarily of New York National Guardsmen.

Valente earned the Medal of Honor for his actions near Ronssoy, France, on 29 September 1918. His Medal of Honor citation reads:

> For conspicuous gallantry and intrepidity above and beyond the call of duty in action with the enemy during the operations against the Hindenburg line, east of Ronssoy, France, 29 September 1918. Finding the advance of his organization held up by a withering enemy machinegun fire, Pvt. Valente volunteered to go forward. With utter disregard of his own personal danger, accompanied by another soldier, Pvt. Valente rushed forward through an intense machinegun fire directly upon the enemy nest, killing 2 and capturing 5 of the enemy and silencing the gun. Discovering another machinegun nest close by which was pouring a deadly fire on the American forces, preventing their advance, Pvt. Valente and his companion charged upon this strong point, killing the gunner and putting this machinegun out of action. Without hesitation they jumped into the enemy's trench, killed 2 and captured 16 German soldiers. Pvt. Valente was later wounded and sent to the rear.[19]

Valente is buried in Long Island National Cemetery in Farmingdale, New York

Born in Cassino, Italy, Pvt. Michael Valente was serving in the 107th Infantry Regiment, 27th Division, when he earned his Medal of Honor. On 29 September, while attacking the Hindenburg Line, Valente repeatedly went forward and destroyed enemy machine gun nests at great risk to his own life. *Courtesy Medal of Honor Society*

**Ludovicus van Iersel (19 October 1893–9 June 1987)**

Sgt. van Iersel was born in Dussen, The Netherlands. He worked as a merchant seaman before enlisting in the US Army. Van Iersel was assigned to Company M of the 9th Infantry Regiment in the 2nd Division. For his valor and personal action at Mouzon, France, he was awarded the Medal of Honor. His Medal of Honor citation reads:

> While a member of the reconnaissance patrol, sent out at night to ascertain the condition of a damaged bridge, Sgt. Van Iersel volunteered to lead a party across the bridge in the face of heavy machinegun and rifle fire from a range of only 75 yards. Crawling alone along the debris of the ruined bridge he came upon a trap, which gave away and precipitated him into the water. In spite of the swift current he succeeded in swimming across the stream and found a lodging place among the timbers on the opposite bank. Disregarding the enemy fire, he made a careful investigation of the hostile position by which the bridge was defended and then returned to the other bank of the river, reporting this valuable information to the battalion commander.[20]

After the war he returned to the United States, became a naturalized citizen, and changed his name to Louis van Iersel. During the Second World War he served with the 3rd Marine Division in the Bougainville Campaign.

**Reidar Waaler (12 February 1894–5 February 1979)**

Sgt. Reidar Waaler was born in Norway. He enlisted in the New York National Guard on 11 June 1917 and was assigned to Company A, 105th Machine Gun Battalion, 27th Division. For his valor near Ronssoy, France, on 27 September 1918, he was awarded the Medal of Honor. His Medal of Honor citation reads:

> In the face of heavy artillery and machinegun fire, he crawled forward to a burning British tank, in which some of the crew were imprisoned, and succeeded in rescuing 2 men. Although the tank was then burning fiercely and contained ammunition which was likely to explode at any time, this soldier immediately returned to the tank and, entering it, made a search for the other occupants, remaining until he satisfied himself that there were no more living men in the tank.[21]

Waaler was also awarded the Distinguished Service Cross, the Montenegrin *Medaille de Bravoure*, the French *Croix de Guerre*, the Italian *Croce di Guerra*, and other Allied country awards for bravery. He is buried in Forest Hills Memorial Park and Mausoleum in Palm City, Florida.

## CHAPTER SEVEN

# THE HOME FRONT

The hyphen will be no more. No matter whence we or our ancestors have come we shall be known hereafter only as Americans, for we have together been baptized in American blood in a common sense.[1]

In any modern war, the line between combat and combat support troops is not always clear-cut, and World War I was no exception. There was no question about frontline infantrymen, machine gunners, artillerymen, and divisional engineers. And most other divisional support troops, such as medical, administrative, supply, and transport troops, were all too often within range of enemy artillery and aircraft.

Farther back, the evacuation hospitals, truck companies, and corps engineer troops also sometimes came under fire. Beyond that, in the intermediate and rear areas there existed a vast "army" of men in purely support roles. From the stevedore, supply, administrative, and transport troops in the port areas to the men in large supply depots in the intermediate zones, these soldiers toiled in generally unglamorous and underappreciated anonymity.

There were a bewildering variety of units in the Services of Supply (SOS)—water supply, railroad operations and maintenance, logging and lumber, and other types of units. These soldiers were just as vital to success as the men with rifles in their hands. Foreign-born soldiers were well represented behind the lines, too. Yet for all the soldiers in uniform, the rules seemed to be understood: a soldier's life in a war zone is fairly well defined by hours of boredom sharply punctuated with minutes of sheer terror. But at least those in uniform have the opportunity to take the fight to the enemy and measure progress by yards won or lost.

On the home front the war was also being waged, not by soldiers, sailors, or Marines, but by their mothers, fathers, wives, children, brothers, sisters, and sweethearts. And it was being waged in deadly earnest. America was a nation at war, and to be seen as anything but 100 percent American was to invite suspicion and investigation.

Those working on the home front to support the AEF in France and the rest of the US Army still in the training camps had no way to take the fight to the enemy.

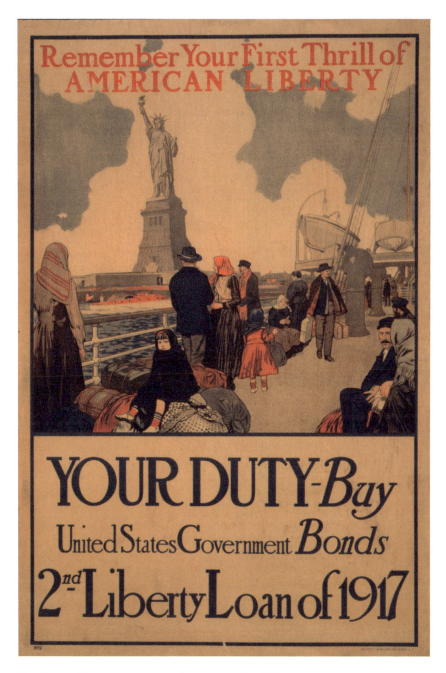

The Statue of Liberty was not only the symbol of the 77th Division—raised from the many ethnic groups living in New York City—it also became a reminder to foreign-born people that they could repay "Lady Liberty's" generosity to them by purchasing war bonds. *Courtesy Library of Congress*

Their efforts, and therefore their war, were measured in tons of coal dug, yards of earth farmed, money raised in bond drives, hours spent guarding key facilities from sabotage, and the less tangible reward of forgoing meat or wheat on certain days.

Sadly, as American efforts in France reached their greatest levels in fall 1918, much of the United States was swept by the Spanish flu. Instead of being able to follow the progress of the massive Meuse-Argonne Offensive, many on the home front were busy trying to find coffins to bury family members who had succumbed to the pandemic. Large cities on the East Coast suffered death rates that would have brought the armies fighting on the Western Front to a halt; nevertheless, they persevered.

Among the more tangible efforts on the home front were the propaganda campaign and the relentless selling of war bonds. A look at the city of Flint, Michigan, is illustrative of the point. There had been some sales of bonds to the foreign-born and immigrant population in the city in the earliest two bond drives, but "it was not until the Third Liberty Loan that a definite organized effort was made to reach those residents of Flint who spoke foreign languages more fluently than English."[2] This time, a foreign-language committee was formed and included community leaders of the different groups who were called "New Americans." The list of some these leaders included such names as Niedzielski, Hamady, Ghitsas, Czerwinski, Menoskey, Goldberger, Kecz, and Cicallo—making the point that there was room for everyone in the bond-buying tent. The members of the committee were responsible for organizing meetings in their areas, as well as ensuring that there were large numbers of New Americans participating in the 6 April 1918 Liberty Day parade.

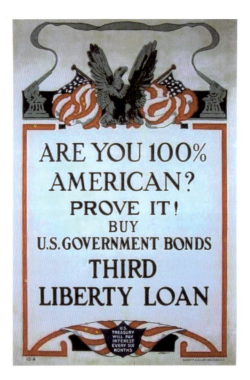

This effort proved so successful that in subsequent bond drives, the language committees continued their efforts and even expanded their charter into developing a program of what they called "Americanization." By the end of the Fifth Bond Drive, they emphasized that buying bonds helped the new arrivals become stockholders investing in America. To the immigrant families, many of whom had brought deeply rooted suspicions of banks from their native lands, this was a powerful message of inclusion in the "American Dream." In time, the dual messages of Amer-

Having used the liberty symbology in previous war bond drives, the Third Bond Drive invoked the challenge of Americanism; the more bonds purchased, the more American you were. *Courtesy National Archives*

Increasing coal production was another way to support the war effort. This poster from the United States Fuel Administration urges digging more coal and employs the languages of the majority of the coal miners: English (Mine More Coal), Italian (*Estraete Sempre Piu'Carbone*), Slovenian (*Koplji Vec Premoga*), Bosnian (*Kopaj Vise Ugljevlja*), Polish (*Starajcie Cie Powiekszyc Produkcje Wegla*), and German (*Foerdert Mehr Kohle*). *Courtesy Virginia War Museum*

icanization and investment were also spread in the local communities of Flint by teachers and school administrators.

Still, there remained issues. The Flint Board of Commerce issued a report stating that the key to the future lay in ensuring that all people from foreign lands received the knowledge and understanding of the "American ideals, traditions and the fundamental principles of democracy." The report continued:

There is a large foreign-born population in the city of Flint, portions of which are more or less isolated from their American friends, many of whom do not speak nor understand our language and who are unfamiliar with American ideals, traditions, and the principles upon which our government is founded.[3]

It became the goal not to only sell bonds, but to help the foreign-born population learn to speak English and make them want to become "true American citizens . . . [and for us] to socialize and humanize [our efforts] in such a way that they can not fail to know our real character, our sense of justice and our sincere desire to guide

Another sign of the intensity of feeling on the home front; this small church has been vandalized because the members of the congregation had not purchased any "Liberty Bonds." With large German American congregations, Lutheran churches were closely watched for anything that might appear to be "anti-American" behavior.

A closer view of the graffiti painted on the front of the building. It repeats the "WE BUY NO BONDS" slogan, then adds, "We love the Kaiser," and the worst insult of the period, "Slackers."

them kindly . . ."[4] Viewed in retrospect that was quite a mission statement, but perhaps now, for the first time, the native-born citizens realized how important it was to reach out and integrate the New Americans. To some extent it happened.

Other cities had experiences similar to Flint's. In many cities and towns the Red Cross played an important role in organizing the "Home-front Army," guiding citizens in everything from teaching first aid to nursing the sick. Local committees were formed to do everything from rolling bandages to knitting for the soldiers. Other typical committees and workgroups conducted secondhand clothing and metal drives. When the Spanish flu epidemic started in fall 1918, the Red Cross took the lead in recruiting nurses and nurses' aides for service in local hospitals and nearby military camps. Foreign-born women willing to serve in these jobs, now dangerous due to increased exposure to the flu, were welcomed; anyone with even a modicum of medical knowledge was desperately needed.

The Salvation Army was one of the most popular support organizations among the soldiers. Both overseas and at home, Salvation Army volunteers worked tirelessly for the benefit of the boys in uniform. The director of the US Salvation Army was Evangeline C. Booth, a native of England. Booth was given the nickname "Commander" because of her strong efforts on behalf of the troops. After the war, the War Department awarded the Distinguished Service Medal to Booth, a tangible indication of the part she and her organization played in the war effort.[5]

Other service organizations were present in large numbers at training camps. Those catering to foreign-born soldiers included the American Library Association, which supplied books in various languages to camps; for example, "Yiddish, Russian, Italian, Romanian, Spanish, and Polish" books were sent to Camp Upton, New York.[6] The Jewish Welfare Board, Knights of Columbus, and Young Men's Christian Association (YMCA) all ministered to foreign-language-speaking soldiers at training camps.[7]

One of the most interesting developments of the stateside war effort was the creation of the Four Minute Men. The wartime Committee on Public Information, seeking ways in which to inform and educate the public, came upon the idea of training and dispersing a number of men who could, in a four-minute time limit, deliver informative speeches to audiences across the country. Often these occurred at movie theaters, following the showing or between double features. The man would appear on stage, give his speech, and depart. Many of these men catered to immigrant communities; speakers delivered speeches in "Italian, Polish, Lithuanian, Magyar-Hungarian, Russian, Ukrainian, Armenian, and Bohemian-Slovak," in addition to Yiddish.[8]

With the National Guard units federalized and either serving in France or preparing to deploy there, the States found themselves without a military organization to provide security and support state or local governments. Minnesota had no large Army training base to call upon for troops should the need arise. As the producer of 16 percent of the world's iron ore and 6 percent of the world's grain, the Minnesota Commission of Public Safety felt the need to protect their vital resources. Accordingly, they created the Minnesota Home Guard and tasked them with protecting public utilities, key bridges, and industrial sites against enemy sabotage. Originally, age limits were set to include men between eighteen and forty-five. Later this would change, as subsequent national drafts in-

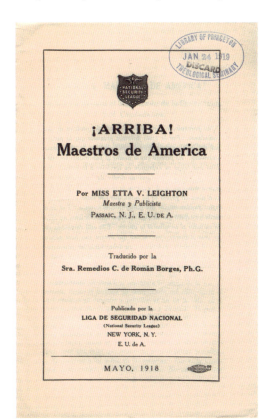

Leaving no stone unturned, the National Security League even published one of their May 1918 pamphlets in Spanish. Addressed to the "Teachers of America," it extolled the virtues of US citizenship. With increasing numbers of immigrants from Spanish-speaking countries, as well as the territories gained after the Spanish-American War, reaching out to these communities made good sense.

cluded those same age parameters. Its mission expanded to fighting fires, escorting drafted men to transportation sites en route to training camps, assisting in the conduct of "slacker raids" to round up deserters or nonregistrants, and assisting in the fight against the flu when it reached epidemic proportions.[9]

It was the same in most states, and once again, many foreign-born men joined in these "home guard" units to do their part. In Virginia, many towns and counties raised volunteer units that were soon incorporated into a State Guard organization. Some of these local companies were included in a larger unit, the Jo Lane Stern Battalion Virginia Volunteers, named after the Virginia state inspector general. Bearing such local names as the Tazewell Rifles, the Russell [County] Guards, the Peaks of Otter Rifles, the Richmond Grays, the Roanoke Machine Works Guard, the Richmond Howitzers, and the Petersburg Guards, the units were equipped with old Krag rifles and whatever uniforms could be obtained. Although most of the officers were established businessmen or local officials, a number of foreign-born men exempted from the draft by age, health, or profession also served in these units. Eventually there were more than thirty such companies statewide, and the last was not deactivated until 1920.[10]

This chapter has only lightly touched on the activities of foreign- and native-born Americans on the home front during the war. With our emphasis on the story of the men and women in uniform, more research into the hard work done on the home front awaits another effort. Returning to our Doughboy focus, the next chapter provides a look at some of the odd and unusual occurrences that took place during the war in the incredibly diverse US military.

## CHAPTER EIGHT

# UNUSUAL EVENTS AND UNIQUE EPISODES

Ten soldiers were billeted in his garret, and while they all solemnly assured him that they were Americans, they spoke no English, nor had they any but the vaguest of ideas about the country they seemed so enthusiastic to fight for. "Am I wrong," he asked, "or do you not all speak English in your United States? And how and why do these little men claim such undying love for a country they know so little of?"[1]

In any in-depth study of military units and military history, there are often a myriad of events that defy easy categorization or refuse to fit smoothly within the rigid constraints of a time line. Often these unusual occurrences or anomalies are so unique or out of the ordinary that some readers might tend to disbelieve them. What follows are some aspects of our story that fall into the unique or unusual category. To the reader tempted to say these must be fiction, the authors fall back on that great military axiom: "You really can't make this stuff up."

**America's Dutch Foreign Legion?**
Among the combat divisions of the AEF, the 4th was known as a highly efficient and capable unit. Remaining in combat almost continuously from July to November 1918, the division built a reputation with solid performances in several campaigns. What also makes the 4th interesting is the surprising number of Dutch-born soldiers within its ranks. In the 39th Infantry Regiment were Pvt. 1st Class Peter Snyer (Zandvoort, North Holland), Cpl. Peter Noordzy (Rotterdam), Pvt. Harm van Horn (Nieuw Beerta), and Pvt. 1st Class Peter Cok (Schore, Zeeland), as well as Pvt. 1st Class Johannes Koopmans, Pvt. William Bothof, and Pvt. 1st Class Sako Ypma, who were listed only as being from the Netherlands. Dutch-born Cpl. Raymond Buma served in the 39th's Machine Gun Company until he was killed in action near Cuisy, in the Verdun sector.

A large number of men from the Netherlands served in the US Army during the war; here is a group of them at one of the many training camps. As best as can be discerned from the handwriting on the back, all these Dutchmen were assigned to the same barracks, and their names are Plien Willenstien, Arie Dibbet, Gerrit Bakker, and Neil Brink. *Courtesy Rogier van de Hoef*

In the 4th Division's 47th Infantry Regiment were Pvt. Bert H. van der Loos (Rotterdam) and Cpl. Edward Otte (Nijmegen), as well as Pvt. Gerrit W. Plaisier, Pvt. 1st Class Eppo Kruize, Pvt. 1st Class Egbertus J. Tonglet, Sgt. Gerrit J. Damveld, and Pvt. 1st Class Gosen Winus Roeten, all of whom are listed simply as being from Holland.

Also serving in the 47th were Pvt. John Paquer (Hoofdplaat), who died of pneumonia in October 1918, and Pvt. Emil Mullaert (IJzendijke), who died of wounds received in August 1918. Another 47th Regiment soldier, Wagoner Dirk Stolk (Barendrecht), survived the war and lived to be 102 years old.

Two more of their fellow Dutch countrymen (Pvt. 1st Class Henry Boorsma and Cpl. Rennie J. Dexter) served in the 58th Infantry Regiment, with twin brothers Herman and Peter Baker originally from Rotterdam. Herman was killed in action in July 1918 and is buried in Aisne-Marne Cemetery in France. In the 59th Infantry Regiment, Cpl. John Henry Remmerden was killed in action during the opening days of the Meuse-Argonne Campaign. Amsterdam-born Marinus Legel was wounded on 7 October 1918, while serving in the 53rd Pioneer Infantry Regiment. Thomas van der Veen served in the 11th Machine Gun Battalion and was awarded the Distinguished Service Cross for "extraordinary heroism in action near Nantillois, France October

10th–13th, 1918 . . . , repeatedly exposing himself to artillery, machine-gun and sniper's fire to deliver important messages . . ."[2]

There were three Dutchmen serving in the 12th Machine Gun Battalion: Pvt. Herman van Steenis, Pvt. George P. Piersma, and Pvt. Anton Luypen.

Cpl. John Noot and Andrew C. Copeman were in the 4th Division's 4th Engineer Regiment. Copeman, whose birth name was Andries Cornelis Koopmans, was from Buitenpost, Achtkarspelen, Friesland, Holland, and was killed in action in July 1918. Another set of brothers were serving in Ambulance Company 19 in the 4th Sanitary train: Henry and Leonard van Ryt. Serving in the 4th Ammunition Train were Wagoner Leo Lammers and Pvt. Jacobus Coltof.

A telling sign of the heavy fighting the 4th Division experienced is that of the thirty-three men listed here, five were killed in action, at least eight more were wounded, and one died of pneumonia, for a casualty rate of just under 50 percent.

With all these hard-fighting, Dutch-born Doughboys, it is perhaps fitting that the 4th Division was chosen to send a detachment of thirty enlisted men and an officer from Company G, 39th Infantry, to serve in Holland after the war.[3]

**What's in a Name? DeLuca for Instance . . .**

The Italian surname DeLuca (also commonly spelled as De Luca) is a common one. With so many Italian immigrants in the United States in 1917–1918, it is not uncommon to find unit rosters of the US Army containing a fair number of men sharing that surname. Archival research bears this out.

The New York State Archives and the Pennsylvania State Archives contain many files that are extremely useful for historians and others seeking more information about foreign-born soldiers serving in the US military.[4] During one such search the surname DeLuca kept appearing repeatedly, daring the historian to dig deeper. Among the many thousands of men who entered the Army and were subsequently credited to New York State was a steady stream of soldiers with that last name.

Cesare DeLuca, originally from Massafra, Italy, served with the 78th Division and was badly wounded near Verdun. Giuseppe DeLuca was also in the 78th Division. Another DeLuca, Dominick, was in the 81st "Wildcat" Division. A second Dominick DeLuca, from Casato, Italy, was wounded in action 27 September 1918, near Vierstadt Ridge, while serving in the 27th Division. Yet a third Dominick served with the 77th Division. Sabino DeLuca from Santa Lucia and Louis DeLuca from Bronte also served in the 77th Division. Serving in the 4th Division was an early volunteer, Sgt. Frank DeLuca, from Rome. Another DeLuca, Lawrence, from Perdifulmo, Salerno, was killed in action just eight days before the armistice while serving in the 2nd Division. There were also DeLucas in the pioneer infantry regiments: Camillo (from Torro) in the 5th and Gaetano in the 51st.

Not all DeLucas were serving in infantry units. There were many in the Army's field artillery regiments: Salvatore (Tagliacozza) was in the 36th Field Artillery, Pasquale (Calabria) was in the 305th Field Artillery, Frank (Naples) was in the 124th Field Artillery, and Bassilio served with the 307th Field Artillery Regiment, while Sabastiano was a wagoner with the 106th Field Artillery. Giuseppe (Penno) and Sabato (Paoline) were in the Coast Artillery Corps.

Some men named DeLuca never made it overseas, including Nicola (Gallichio) with the 48th Infantry Regiment and Charles (Naples) in the 58th Field Artillery Regiment. Giovanni (Penno) served in the 157th Depot Brigade at Camp Gordon. Michael DeLuca (Lucerna) served at Camp Upton and Fort Slocum, while Micke DeLuca served on the staff of the Machine Gun Training Center at Camp Hancock, near Augusta, Georgia. Joseph DeLuca (Tioro Patti) served at Camp Vail, New Jersey, and Camp Sevier. Another Joseph DeLuca, who only listed Italy as his birthplace, served at Camp Upton until his November 1917 discharge for a physical disability.

Antonio (Attansio) DeLuca served at Camp Wadsworth, South Carolina, until his death from tuberculosis in October 1918. In 1934, Antonio's widowed mother filed a claim from Italy via the American Legion post in Rome for compensation from Pennsylvania on the basis of the service of her son. The claim was denied on the basis of the result of a residence review board that concluded that Antonio had not resided in Pennsylvania, but New York, when he entered the Army.

Pennsylvania's archives revealed some twenty-eight Italian-born DeLucas, plus one born in Canada. Of these twenty-nine men, twenty served overseas and nine served stateside. They served in a variety of units, including infantry, field artillery, coast artillery, trench mortar, engineer, supply, and medical units. One man, Rocco DeLuca, served in the 831st Aero Squadron overseas; Tony DeLuca was a bugler for

Pvts. Gaetano DeLuca, Anthony Scalero, and Luigi Clemenza, all Italian-born men serving in the 51st Pioneer Infantry Regiment. The 51st was originally built around the New York National Guard's 10th Infantry Regiment but later included a large number of foreign-born soldiers. The regiment was part of the Army of Occupation after the war and was assigned to the US IV Corps. *Courtesy NYDMNA*

Troop I, 1st Cavalry Regiment, in the United States; Joseph DeLuca served in US Ambulance Service Section 596 in Italy; and nineteen-year-old Anthony DeLuca was in the Students' Army Training Corps at the University of Pennsylvania.

Dominick DeLuca of the 37th Division was killed in action during the Meuse-Argonne Offensive. Giuseppe DeLuca of the 42nd Division died of wounds received in action in October 1918. Three other DeLucas were wounded in action: Domenico DeLuca; Luigi DeLuca, 28th Division (gas and shrapnel); and Anthony DeLuca, 80th Division (gassed). The precise fate of another, Aniello DeLuca, serving in the 212th Military Police Company in the AEF, is uncertain. Aniello's compensation applications lists "Amputation thigh, left middle third." Four other Pennsylvania DeLucas received discharges during their training due to physical disability issues.

A check of the Utah archives reveals only one DeLuca: Antonio, who was wounded in action with the 42nd Division. Ohio records reveal four DeLuca men serving: three overseas and one stateside. Nick DeLuca, in the 3rd Division, was wounded and cited for gallantry in action.

So what can be derived from this admittedly unscientific survey of foreign-born soldiers named DeLuca, credited to several different states? Interestingly enough, even with this small sample size, they appear to match the overall statistics of the US Army of the First World War. Of approximately sixty soldiers, two were killed in action, one died of wounds, one died of disease, about six were severely wounded, and five were discharged while in training camp due to physical disability. As with the US Army of the period, the preponderance of DeLucas were serving in infantry and artillery units, while support units, such as signal and transportation, are slightly represented. The only deviation from the overall picture is that two-thirds of the DeLucas—some forty men—served in France while twenty remained in the States. For the overall Army, the percentage split was closer to fifty/fifty.

**Brothers in Service**

If one considers that more than four million men served in the US military during World War I, then there must have been thousands of sets of brothers—foreign and US born—serving at the same time. Examples abound, but one case study of three Italian-born brothers will reflect what must have been fairly commonplace. The three Pellegrini brothers—Pasquale (Charles, born 1890), Francesco (Frank, born 1892), and Luigi (Louis, born 1896)—had been trained as tailors in Italy by their father, Saverio. The young men made their way to the United States and joined their oldest brother, Pietro, in his tailoring business in Chicago.[5]

The brothers were proud of their adopted country. Charles became a US citizen in 1914 and at some point briefly served in the Illinois National Guard. In January 1917, Louis ventured to Fort Sam Houston, near San Antonio, Texas, and enlisted in Company E, 4th Illinois Infantry Regiment, serving there as part of the Mexican border patrol.

After the US declaration of war, Charles and Frank registered for the draft, and Louis, now a bugler in Company E, departed for Camp Logan, Texas, with his regiment, which was soon redesignated as the 130th Infantry Regiment, 33rd Division.

Charles Pellegrini (standing, center) with other Italian American soldiers in a portrait made during stateside training in 1918. Pellegrini served in the 56th Infantry Regiment, 7th Division. His brothers Louis and Frank also served in the US Army during the war. *Courtesy Andrea Koprcina McGuire*

Louis and the 33rd sailed for France in May 1918. From their arrival until mid-August, when they were finally assigned to the AEF, the men of the 33rd Division served and trained with the British and Australians, and Louis served his apprenticeship in the trenches.

While Louis was training in the United States, his brothers were drafted, and both reported for duty on 2 May 1918. They were sent to Camp MacArthur, near Waco, Texas, where they were assigned to the newly formed 7th Division. Charles was assigned to the 56th Infantry Regiment; Frank, to the 55th Infantry Regiment. The division departed for Camp Merritt, New Jersey, in July. At Camp Merritt, Frank took advantage of the opportunity afforded to alien US soldiers and became a US citizen. It is unclear whether Charles went overseas with his regiment; extant service records, which show no overseas service, clash with family lore that claims Charles went overseas and was badly gassed. It is known that brother Frank did go overseas with the 7th Division.

After arrival, the 7th Division moved into the line in the Lorraine sector; at the same time Louis and the 33rd Division prepared to begin the Meuse-Argonne Offensive. The 33rd Division was the right flank unit of the US First Army, with its own

Bugler Louis Pellegrini of the 130th Infantry Regiment, 33rd Division, in a portrait made while training at Camp MacArthur, Texas. Pellegrini was gassed during the Meuse-Argonne Offensive as the 33rd Division struggled to rid the west bank of the Meuse of German and Austrian artillery. He was later awarded the Purple Heart. *Courtesy Mark Koprcina and Andrea Koprcina McGuire*

Frank Pellegrini of the 55th Infantry Regiment, 7th Division. Pellegrini saw combat as part of the 2nd Army during the closing month of the war. This photograph was taken in France and gives a very clear picture of the amount of equipment each Doughboy carried into battle. *Courtesy Andrea Koprcina McGuire*

right flank resting on the Meuse River. On 29 September, the 33rd occupied the front line in the tangled growth of the Bois de la Cote Lemont. Louis and Company E took up support positions with two companies on the north edge of Bois d'en Dela and two companies in Bois de Septsarges.

While in this position in the woods near the bend in the Meuse, Louis and his comrades suffered badly from shelling and gas attacks. They were raked by machine gun and artillery fire from their front and from areas across the Meuse River to the east. On 11 October, Louis was gassed and evacuated to a hospital.

At about the same time, Frank was undergoing similar experiences near the St. Mihiel sector. The 7th Division had been assigned to the new American Second Army in that area and was preparing to begin an offensive directed toward the Metz area scheduled for November. By mid-October, Frank, along with the 55th Infantry Regiment, had held the line against machine gun, artillery, and gas attacks. On 8 November, they participated in an attack against severe artillery and machine gun fire which, despite casualties, successfully netted a large number of prisoners, weapons, and ammunition. The men in the 7th Division were notified of the armistice the morning of 11 November, just hours before it was to take effect. For the rest of the fall and into winter, Frank and the others of his regiment were engaged in salvage work in the area, reclaiming, categorizing, and storing vast quantities of excess or abandoned government materiel.

Charles received his discharge at Camp Grant at the end of December 1918. Meanwhile, Louis convalesced in hospitals until his return to the United States in March 1919; he was discharged that same month. Frank followed in June 1919, and by that summer the Pellegrini brothers were once again together with their family.

The brothers traded their rifles, revolvers, and grenades for scissors, tape measures, and cloth, resuming their successful tailoring business. Their story is a microcosm of the "American Dream" in the eyes of many immigrants of the day. Coming from a foreign nation, they established themselves in business, became US citizens, served in the American Army in a time of war, and returned home to resume their business and start a family.

## The Japanese Anomaly at Camp Upton (Winter 1917)

One of the many interesting quandaries the US military establishment faced in 1917 was the fact that if universal conscription was truly universal, it would be necessary to draft groups of men previously not considered eligible or desirable for military service. Even postwar AGO Forms 724-1 and 724-2, meant to document a soldier's service, had only two racial categories: "White" and "Colored." So what was to be done with men drafted from Japan, Korea, China, or other Asian countries?[6]

A study of the service cards found in the New York files for drafted men from Japan shows that because there was no clear-cut answer or guidance, it fell to the individual draft board clerk to figure it out. Ultimately the clerks documented most of these men as Japanese, White, or Yellow.

Perhaps of greater interest was the fact that there appears to have been an ingrained bias against Japanese men drafted in the state of New York. In almost every case where an inductee was ordered to report to Camp Upton on Long Island, he would eventually be discharged from the service for a multitude of reasons, including "Convenience of Gov't" (Fukuzo Hashimoto and Kunihei Murabe), "Request of Japanese Minister" (Kozno Hiraiwa), "account of being Japanese citizen" (Kameichi Kato), and "Subject of Japan" (Kaoru Matsuyama). What makes this anomaly so striking is that drafted Japanese men sent to other camps established a very good record of service: Pvt. 1st Class Yasusaburo Kasagi and Pvt. Joseph Tomanaga served honorably in France with the 59th Pioneer Infantry Regiment; Goro Kogoshima was promoted to corporal while serving with the 323rd Infantry Regiment, 81st Division; and George T. Nakamura was promoted to private 1st class while serving with a medical unit in France. Ironically, Japanese-born Taro Sahara would serve honorably in the US Navy on the USS *President Grant* in the First World War, only to be sent to a Japanese internment camp during the Second World War.

So what can be made of this? Were certain men, perhaps favored by the Japanese government for political or business reasons, sent to Camp Upton to ensure they would not be sent overseas? Or was there a group of US Army administrators at Camp Upton determined to keep Japanese men out of the army? This last option seems hardly plausible because Camp Upton was administered by Maj. Gen. J. Franklin Bell, one of the more vocal supporters of African American soldiers training there. He was also a supporter of naturalizing foreign-born men to allow them to serve. In a strange twist to this story, Chinese men also drafted in New York and sent to Camp Upton do not appear to have been affected by the factors previously mentioned. As evidenced by the service records of Jun Chan, Ly Tung, Wong Ming Gin, Hang Hong, Wong Foo, and others, the Chinese draftees appeared to have navigated the induction system and the Camp Upton training regimen without incident.

## An Officer and a Gentleman (May 1919)

It is somewhat surprising that with all the fuss and activity surrounding the drafting of immigrants—friendly or enemy—very little attention was paid to the fact that there were already a large number of foreign-born officers in the US Army. It was not until May 1919, when the Regular Army published its master list of officers, that someone noticed 259 of the officers on the list were "born under flags other than that of the United States." The *New York Times* reported that 136 had been born in British Commonwealth countries (England, Canada, Scotland, Wales, South Africa, India, and Ireland), 32 were born in Germany, 11 in Austria, and 16 in Russia. Scandinavia contributed twelve from Sweden, six from Norway, and three from Finland. The highest-ranking foreign-born US officer was Brig. Gen. Robert J. Fleming, a cavalryman born in Ireland.[7]

**A Mexican Doughboy Tells His Story**

Mexican-born Manuel B. Gonzales volunteered to serve in "la guerra encontra el Alemania" (the war against Germany) and was sent to Camp Funston in April 1918.[8] He was trained as part of the 354th Infantry Regiment, 89th Division, and sent to Camp Mills for overseas movement. At the transit camp Gonzales underwent a medical operation and remained there when the 89th departed. Finally healed, on 19 July 1918, Pvt. Gonzales wrote home:

> My Dearest Mother, May this letter find you in good health . . . Don't be sad because I am going to say goodbye to you and my brothers. I don't know if this will be my [last] thoughts because I don't know if I will have difficulties at sea. . . . And if God helps us during our crossing at sea, I will always write as long as God grants me life because I carry you in my heart.
>
> Mother, my eyes have misted but not because I regret. . . . What I regret the most is that I didn't send my picture, so that you can have me with my gun on a corner table for all to see how it's done when someone wants to be a man, with deeds and not words.[9]

After arrival in France, Gonzales later wrote that he and his comrades spent sleepless days and nights in famous 40/8 railcars as they were transported to a training camp for more tactical instruction. By September, Gonzales was assigned to the 306th

Mexican-born Manuel B. Gonzales wears a somber look as he poses for a portrait in a French studio. Originally assigned to the 89th Division, he was later assigned to the 306th Field Signal Battalion, supporting the 81st Division. *Courtesy New Mexico Commission of Public Records, State Records Center and Archives*

Field Signal Battalion of the 81st Division. Soon thereafter, in the St. Dies sector, they began their mission of providing signal support to the division.

A short while later, Gonzales, the 81st Division, and most of the AEF became involved in the Meuse-Argonne Offensive. He wrote vividly of the constant rain and all-night German artillery barrages. After the armistice, Gonzales was promoted to private 1st class and then to the rank of cook. In May 1919, he and his comrades were sent to the departure port St. Nazaire. After loading on the *Roanoke*, they sailed to Charleston, South Carolina, and from there went to Camp Jackson for demobilization. The camaraderie of the Army in general and his unit in particular appealed to Gonzales, and he wrote that "Mi corazón sintio tristeza por que me separaba de mis buenos officiales y de mis compañeros de tantos suffrimientos." ("My heart was sad to know that it would be separated from my good officers and my comrades of much shared suffering.") From Jackson, Gonzales was sent to Fort Bliss, Texas, to be closer to his home when he was finally discharged in July 1919. He signed his final personal testimony with the simple words: "Libertad y Gloria."

**You Can't Always Get What You Want**
Most soldiers had at least some desire for overseas service. Many enlisted before being drafted, in the hopes of early deployment to France. Such zeal did not always pay off. Frank Gouin, a native of Winnipeg, Canada, was a twenty-three-year-old college graduate working as a petroleum geologist when he entered officers training camp at Leon Springs, Texas, on 17 July 1917.

Commissioned as a second lieutenant in the field artillery, he accepted a transfer to the Army Air Service with the promise of imminent overseas service. He was assigned to the 240th Aero Squadron at Kelly Field, Texas, on 27 December 1917. The War Department then appeared to go back on its promise; Gouin was "relieved of duty with this squadron when it was ordered overseas two weeks later, as were all other line officers who had transferred to the Air Service with the promise of immediate overseas service."[10]

For the next seven months Gouin served in various positions with cadet squadrons. As he later wrote, "By this time [I] had had enough of non-combatant work so on request to return to the Field Artillery was recommissioned as a 2nd Lieut, F.A. on

The service record for Raghunath Banawalker. Living in New York City, it was almost a foregone conclusion that he would serve in the 77th Division. The 77th was composed almost entirely of draftees from New York City and was the first National Army division to deploy to France. *Courtesy New York State Abstracts of World War I Military Service, 1917–1919*

July 22, 1918 . . .”[11] Gouin attended more training before finally receiving orders for overseas service on 25 October 1918. Held at Camp Jackson, South Carolina, to await the arrival of other "casual" officers, Gouin never made it overseas: "Armistice too close on our heels so Nov. 11 found us still there." And there Gouin stayed until his discharge on 6 December. Frank Gouin, zealous volunteer for immediate overseas service, spent his eighteen months of wartime service in the United States.

Not all foreign-born men were enthusiastic about joining the US Army. In this case, Abdul Samad registered for the draft but did not report to his induction station. Considered a "deserter" by the Army, Samad was finally found and turned over to the authorities at nearby Camp Upton. Samad was then assigned to the 329th Service Battalion, an African American unit, and sent to France to work in the Services of Supply. *Courtesy New York State Abstracts of World War I Military Service, 1917–1919*

Ship's Cook 4th Class Heppocrates Belmegis was born in Turkey but was living in Rochester when he joined the Navy in June 1918. He reported for training at Pelham Bay Park, New York, but was there less than a month before he became sick and died of pneumonia on 10 October 1918. *Courtesy New York State Archives and Rochester and Monroe County, New York*

## An Italian in the Rainbow Division

With the declaration of war in 1917, Nicholas Martone and his friends decided to join the New York National Guard. Thinking it would simplify the process, Martone lied and said he was born in the United States. He was assigned to the 69th Infantry Regiment, later the 165th Infantry Regiment, and became part of New York's contribution to the 42nd "Rainbow" Division. Assigned to Camp Mills, he could go home at night and eat with his family. This was a double blessing, because in common with many new soldiers, he did not like Army food. That interlude ended when the 42nd Division departed for France, sailing from Hoboken to Brest.

Martone's earliest impressions of France were not particularly favorable, since the soldiers of his units were forced to make a four-day hike through deep snow. On arrival at their destination, artillery fire could be heard in the distance, and they knew they were near the front. Eventually the division took over a section of the trenches on the Champagne front. On 15 July, they found themselves in the midst of an extremely heavy artillery battle that pounded both sides of the front line. When his unit withdrew from the front, Martone recalled that as they marched to the rear, they saw a "Polish Regiment, all killed by German Artillery fire." Later, while serving on the Ourq River front, he received a letter from his mother informing him that he had been drafted by the Italian Army.[12]

A short while later, Martone was part of a patrol dispatched to find and kill a German sniper who had been picking off Americans. The patrol was considered so dangerous that the Canadian-born regimental chaplain Father Francis P. Duffy came over and gave the soldiers absolution. The mission proved unsuccessful, but Martone returned safely.

By 11 October 1918, Martone was engaged in the Meuse-Argonne Offensive. Once again he was involved in anti-sniper patrolling, but his luck ran out; he was wounded

when his patrol came under fire from both sides. Fortunately the Americans ceased fire when they recognized the shape of the Doughboys' helmets. Martone and his wounded comrades were taken to a hospital in Tours. After the shrapnel was removed from his leg, Martone was quite happy to find that the doctor had saved it for him as a souvenir. He was also very happy to be in a clean, warm hospital ward, since the weather had turned increasingly bad.

Ultimately, he was given a choice between returning to his regiment or returning to the States on a casualty ship. He chose to rejoin his unit, but the US Army changed his mind

John (Giovanni) Bressan, a native of Italy and a blacksmith by trade, served in the US Navy as a blacksmith, 1st class, at the North Island Aviation Station in California from January 1918 to February 1919. *Utah, Military Records, 1862–1970*

for him, and after placing him in charge of training some new arrivals, he was soon on a ship headed back to the States.

**Literacy in the Army (1917–1919)**
Early in the conscription and Army-building process it was recognized that many recently arrived foreign-born soldiers could not read, write, speak, or understand English. There was also a problem with foreign-born soldiers who had lived in the United States for quite some time but were still far from fluent in English.

One study explained that this part of the literacy problem stemmed from the fact that some soldiers had "lived in colonies composed almost wholly of people of their own nationality, and, lacking the actual need of English, they failed to learn it."[13] What did turn out to be somewhat of a surprise was the fairly large number of native-born US soldiers who could neither read nor write English. The same report recorded that "Some of the men who come from the remote mountain districts of this country are also unable either to read or to write."[14] A telling sign of the level of this problem for the native-born soldiers was the number of men who, on reaching their first training camp, thought they were now in France.

The American Army criterion for judging literacy at the time was the ability to read and understand a newspaper, and to write a letter that could be read and understood by an ordinary, literate man. Later studies revealed that at least 4 percent of the native-born soldiers in the US Army could not pass this test. On the basis of this standard, Pershing was commanding a force in France with some 50,000 illiterate native-born soldiers and perhaps 250,000 foreign-born soldiers with varying degrees of literacy.[15] The numbers for the Army still in training in the States were even higher because it was a larger force.

Events would later show that many of the problems arising with the AEF in France, and later during the occupation of Germany, could be laid at the door of illiteracy. An After-Action Report recorded:

> illiterates are exceptionally dangerous during the occupation of a foreign country, in as much as they are incapable of amusing themselves in a better way during their leisure hours and are apt to give way to self-indulgence and dissipation.[16]

So what was to be done? Working with education specialists, the Army developed a series of books to teach reading and impart military and citizenship values. Among the most notable was the *Soldier's First Book* by Cora Wilson Stewart, whose experience in teaching reading and writing to illiterate southerners had prepared her for the challenge.

Using humor, her lessons were meant to impart a meaningful understanding of English that would help the soldier to better understand and obey orders. The unexpectedly quick ending of the war in November 1918 meant that many of the soldiers still in training in stateside camps were discharged back into civilian life without having gained much in the way of knowledge of the English language, and many would still sign their final paperwork by making their "mark."[17]

## The Danish West Indies

Most Americans have forgotten that the beautiful vacation destination known as the US Virgin Islands once belonged to Denmark, and were bought in 1917 for twenty-five million dollars. Unlike Puerto Rico, Alaska, and Hawaii, the long arm of the Conscription Act did not reach out to the Virgin Islands. Possibly it was an oversight, or perhaps the US provost marshal's office running the draft boards did not want to take on the sticky problem of how to define citizenship of the islands' inhabitants.

Only months earlier, the population had been citizens of neutral Denmark and were now living in a US territory. Ultimately, it did not much matter; men from any of the West Indies or nearby Caribbean islands living in the United States were subject to draft registration and potential service in the US military.

A survey of draft registration records reveals a phenomenal variety of birth locations: British West Indies, Dutch West Indies, Danish West Indies, the Grenadines, Jamaica, Antigua, St. Kitts, Barbados, Grenada, St. Vincent, St. Lucia, Nassau, Tobago, Dominica, and Montserrat. The racial categorizations are equally varied: African, Ethiopian, Black, Colored, Hindu, White, Caucasian, Negro, East Indian, Malayan, and even "Jamaican Blood."[18]

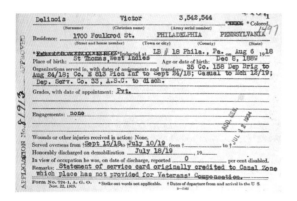

The WWI service record for Pvt. Victor Delinois, born on the island of St. Thomas in the Danish West Indies (US Virgin Islands). Victor served in the 813th Pioneer Infantry Regiment in France after training at Camp Sherman, Ohio. *Courtesy Pennsylvania Archives*

## India's Contribution to the American Army

With India having been the largest and most important British colony for many years, it is not surprising that many Indians served in the British Army during the First World War. What is surprising is the number of India-born men serving in the US Army. It is hard to pin down the actual total, since the numbers are inflated by the inclusion of American citizens who, as children of missionaries, were also born in India. It is the same with the numbers from China, in that a great number of missionaries' offspring were born in that country.

Adding to the confusion is the tendency of the draft board clerks filling out the registration cards to make mistakes. Often "India" is written "Indiana" and vice versa.

Equally common is the use of "Indies" instead of "India." However, a review of draft registration records shows over a thousand men named Singh (a common Indian surname) registered for the draft. Obviously some of these were American-born children of immigrants.

More to our purpose, there were several thousand men who listed India as their birthplace while registering to be in compliance with the Conscription Act. Among that number was Ragunath N. Banawalker, a twenty-five-year-old man from Bombay, India, living in New York City. Pvt. Banawalker was inducted in the Army in February 1918 and assigned to the 305th Field Artillery Regiment. Less than two months later he was in France serving as a medic in the 305th Infantry Regiment. By October, he had served on the Baccarat and Vesle fronts, and in the Oise-Aisne Campaign. Shortly after Banawalker and the 305th rescued the "Lost Battalion" in the Argonne, he was wounded. By the time he returned home, Banawalker had served over a year in France, most of it in combat operations.

From Lackawanna, New York, came Wali Muhommad. Originally from Pessawar, India, Muhommad enlisted in the New York National Guard in July 1917 and was assigned to Battery A of the 106th Field Artillery, 27th Division. He served with the 106th throughout the war and was then assigned to the 299th Military Police Company. Promoted to private 1st class, Muhommad remained in France until August 1919, when he returned to the States and was demobilized.

Another New York City resident from Bombay, Kekee Patell was inducted into the Army in June 1918 and sent to Camp Hancock, Georgia, for machine gun training. Just two months later he was in France, serving in the 148th Machine Gun Battalion. Yet another Bombay-born man, Sam Hindo, was inducted in April 1918 and assigned to the 367th Infantry Regiment in the African American 92nd Division, participating in the Meuse-Argonne Offensive.

Sadek Ali Mollah, from Hoogli, Bengal, India, was inducted in August 1918 and died from the Spanish flu/bronchopneumonia in his training camp in October 1918. More fortunate was Minoo Phiroze, who enlisted in the Regular Army in June 1917 and spent the duration of the war in the States, serving in the 23rd and 4th Cavalry Regiments. Pvt. 1st Class Phiroze must have enjoyed military life, since he remained in the Army until 1920.

Perhaps most illustrative of the service of India-born men are the records of three men with the last name Singh who were credited to New York. Gordit Singh enlisted in the Regular Army in August 1917 and was assigned to the 23rd Infantry Regiment, 2nd Division. Pvt. 1st Class Singh served with that elite unit until February 1919, when he was discharged with a 10 percent disability. Harnam Singh was drafted in April 1918 and sent to Camp Johnston, Florida, for training. From there he went to Camp Sill, Oklahoma, and served in the Motor Transport Corps until the end of the war. By the time he was discharged he had been promoted to corporal. Dytiari Singh was drafted in July 1918, and after training at Camp Upton he was transferred to Camp Hancock, Georgia, for service in the Army Ordnance Corps. In February 1919 he was discharged from the terms of his original enlistment so he could reenlist in the Regular Army.[19]

**Syrians and Others . . .**

Judging by documents pertaining to Pennsylvania World War I veterans, men classified as having been born in Syria actually came from a number of areas, including Jerusalem, Lebanon, Palestine, Turkey, and Tripoli. In particular, men born in Turkey sometimes had "Syria, Turkey" as their birthplace. This haphazard method of categorizing men from "Syria" makes it very difficult to extrapolate information for specific national or ethnic groups covered under the "Syria" generalization. Perhaps the best that can be said, at least in the case of Pennsylvania Syrians, is that most of them were born within the Ottoman Empire. Many of the men's names are anglicized; thus, we find such surnames as Abbott, Brody, and Corey, which might more accurately be Abed, Baroody, and Khouri.

A total of 115 men from Pennsylvania were identified as having been born in Syria. Of these, sixty-four served stateside only, while fifty-one served overseas. It is not known how many of the men were US citizens at the time of their enlistment, but many clearly were not. Thirteen of the men were discharged because of their status as an enemy alien, including two men for "erroneous induction."

Harry S. Abbott and Tony S. Abbutt, both living at the same address in Pittsburgh, were drafted and reported for duty on 23 September 1917. Harry served in a machine gun unit, the Ordnance Corps, a remount unit, and two depot brigades stateside before his discharge as an enemy alien on 8 January 1919, two months after war's end. Tony, who was quite possibly Harry's brother, served in the 315th Machine Gun Battalion at Camp Lee before his discharge for "erroneous induction" on 20 November 1917.

Eight of the men were discharged during their training on a Surgeon's Certificate of Disability; their disability ranged from 10 to 25 percent. Among the 115 men, most enlisted ranks were represented, including cook, mechanic, wagoner, and bugler. The highest rank was achieved by First Sgt. Ayoup S. Hatem, Company A, 310th Machine Gun Battalion, 79th Division.

The men served in the full array of World War I Army units, including infantry, artillery, engineer, air service, cavalry, medical, transportation, and other support units. Curiously, eight of the men served in the 111th Infantry Regiment, 28th Division.

Of note is the fact that thirty-four men enlisted either in the Regular Army (twenty-two men) or the National Guard (twelve men). Some enlisted before the war. Pvt. Thomas G. Eleam enlisted in March 1915 and served in the Philippines and on the Mexican border. Sgt. Ayoup S. Hatem enlisted in 1911 and served in the Philippines with Company I, 13th Infantry Regiment, from 1911 to 1914. Cpl. Charles Thomas also served in the Philippines with the 13th from 1915 to 1917.

Pvt. 1st Class Pete Mike enlisted in the Pennsylvania National Guard on 6 January 1917. After training with the National Guard, and upon the Guard's federalization, Mike was assigned to Company H, 111th Infantry Regiment, 28th Division. Mike's death while serving with the regiment was reported by an eyewitness: "Killed by shell fire about 2PM, July 16th [1918], just to the right of Crezancy. Death was instantaneous. He was buried on the spot."

Thirteen men were wounded or gassed in action, and one other was injured in the line of duty. The wounded men were Pvt. 1st Class Thomas A. Corry, 111th Infantry

Regiment, 28th Division (gunshot wound, 3 October 1918); Pvt. Leo David, 117th Sanitary Train, 42nd Division (gassed); Pvt. David Elias, 319th Infantry Regiment, 80th Division (wounded 10 October 1918); Pvt. Farris Fraed, 59th Infantry Regiment, 4th Division (severely wounded 31 July 1918); Pvt. Sam Hemett, 111th Infantry Regiment, 28th Division (shrapnel, 10 August 1918); Pvt. 1st Class Sam Isaac, 23rd Infantry Regiment, 2nd Division (gassed); Pvt. Peter Iseral, 26th Infantry Regiment, 1st Division (wounded 20 July 1918); Pvt. Louis Joibur, 26th Infantry Regiment, 1st Division ("Shell Shocked, Gassed, Shrapnel left foot," 4 June 1918); Pvt. Nicola E. Joseph, 111th Infantry Regiment, 28th Division (gunshot wound, 11 August 1918); Pvt. Sam Kasem, 319th Infantry Regiment, 80th Division ("Shrapnel in right shoulder," 10 October 1918); Pvt. Mike B. Kassab 319th Infantry Regiment, 80th Division ("Severe gun shot wound in left arm," 9 October 1918); Pvt. 1st Class Albert Mike, 320th Infantry Regiment, 80th Division (gassed); Pvt. Elias Sowan, 111th Infantry Regiment, 28th Division (gassed, 21 July 1918); and Pvt. John Joseph, 6th Cavalry Regiment (injured "back, right wrist, left ear," August 1918, while serving overseas).[20]

**Join the Navy and See the World**

Although the Navy never grew nearly as large as the Army, its size did increase, and a good number of the new sailors were born in other countries. The Navy's role in the First World War is often wrongly overlooked and is worthy of an in-depth study.

Far beyond just battling German and Austro-Hungarian U-boats, the Navy conducted a very effective convoy system, created a series of large-scale naval facilities in Europe and the United States, participated in laying the massive North Sea minefield, and even provided aviation support to the front lines. When the war was over, the Navy turned much of its efforts and many of its ships to bringing the AEF back to America. Among its greatest accomplishments was that not one Doughboy, either being carried on a US Navy ship or on a ship with US Navy escorts, lost his life due to enemy action while crossing the Atlantic.

**The Army Gets It Right**

Sometimes the Army wisely made use of the skills a man possessed prior to his enlistment. Bruno Lange, a twenty-three-year-old native of Germany, had attended high school and business schools in Utah before his enlistment on 18 October 1917. Lange possessed seven years of practical business experience and was employed as an accountant with a savings institution at the time.

Initially assigned to the infantry, Lange was quickly reassigned to detached service at Fort McPherson, Georgia, and then to Washington, DC, where he served as a company clerk and post exchange bookkeeper. Lange was initially recommended as a candidate for an officers training course, but he was disqualified for a physical defect. Later he was recommended for a direct commission as a second lieutenant in the Quartermaster Corps, but the armistice intervened and he was not commissioned. Lange was discharged in September 1919.

One of Lange's brothers, Hans, also had administrative abilities that he used in military service. Hans Lange served as a stenographer in the personnel office of the

145th Field Artillery Regiment, 40th Division. A third brother, Carl, served in the Coast Artillery in 1918.[21]

Another interesting case of matching skills and abilities with military requirements is that of Gennaro Striano, a twenty-six-year-old native of Italy who served in Section 601, American Army Ambulance Service, in Italy. Striano was a clergyman and a student at the Divinity School of the Protestant Episcopal Church of Philadelphia when he was granted a leave of absence to enlist as an interpreter on 17 April 1918. Promoted to sergeant on 4 June, Striano was sent overseas a month later. While in Italy, he participated in the Vittorio Veneto Campaign; after the war he was promoted to sergeant 1st class.[22]

## Where Exactly Is Albania, Albania?

Many of the draft boards and military training centers had trouble defining some countries of origin, such as Macedonia, on the men's registration cards. It was the same for Albania. Having been an independent country only since 1914, men with Albanian birthplaces can be found listed as coming from Albania, Italy; Albania, Turkey; Albania, Greece; even Albania, Albania; or just Albania.[23] Perhaps surprisingly for such a small country, there were at least twenty-four Albanians who entered the Army from New York State and another fifty from Pennsylvania.

Abraham Kasso, born in Albania in 1892, had more than enough reasons to want to fight against the Germans and their Turkish allies; Turks killed his father in the Second Balkan War and burned his mother alive in 1912. Kasso was trained as an Army engineer at Camp Humphreys and was naturalized there on 11 July 1918, before deploying to France. *Courtesy Genesee County, Michigan, Archives*

The numbers appear about evenly split between men who served only in the States and men who deployed to France. Among those with the AEF were Lambi Chala (born in Desnitsi, Albania) with the 346th Infantry, 87th Division; John Dalip (Korcha, Albania) with the 312th Infantry, 78th Division; Pvt. 1st Class Peter Efthim (Albania, Albania) and Ilia Zografo (Kartsa, Albania) with the 309th Infantry, 78th Division; Charles Korcha (Coritza, Albania) with the 1st Provisional Labor Battalion; Christy Lara (Korcha, Albania), who was part of a replacement draft from Camp Gordon to the 161st Infantry, 41st Division; Cpl. Louis Nassy (Albania), who served with several motor transport companies and remained in France until December 1919; George Naum (Biliste, Albania, Greece), who served with the 312th Infantry, 78th Division, and was severely wounded near Champignuelle on 18 October 1918; Refat Suleiman (Albania), who served with the 347th Infantry, 87th Division; Naum Vasal (Albania), who served with the 59th Pioneer Infantry Regiment; and Pvt. 1st Class

Janero Sico (San Sofia, Albania), who served with the 1st Pioneer Infantry Regiment until his death from the Spanish flu in September 1918.

## The Navy Gets It Right

The Navy, undergoing a rapid expansion just like the Army, soon found it required the services of men with special skills. With the large influx of men into training camps came problems with repairing and altering tens of thousands of uniforms issued to the recruits. Accordingly, the Navy recruited men with tailoring skills; some of the respondents were foreign-born tailors. Three Italian-born men were among those who enlisted as tailors in the Navy. Eugenio Ferraro, Anthony Spizzirri, and Louis Bruno all were born in Marano Marchesato, a small village in the southern Italian region of Calabria; all three were part of the migration pattern from that village to Chicago and Kenosha, Wisconsin, that began in the late 1870s. All three served at Great Lakes Naval Training Station, a major induction and training base then and now, about forty-five miles due north of Chicago and twenty miles south of Kenosha.

Eugenio Ferraro was born in 1893, and he came to the United States in 1910 to join his brothers in Kenosha.[24] On 11 April 1918, Ferraro filed his declaration of intention to become a US citizen; the next day he journeyed twenty miles south to Great Lakes Naval Training Station, where he enlisted in the Navy, with special duty as a tailor. He was given the rating fireman, 1st class—a higher-than-normal rating for most recruits, granted almost certainly because of his skill as a tailor.[25] He became a naturalized US citizen at Great Lakes on 2 July 1918.[26]

Ferraro served his entire stint in the US Navy at Great Lakes, where "he basically worked as a tailor in the Navy," performing alterations and repairs for the thousands of wartime recruits flooding the station. It was like "a regular job; after basic training he didn't live on base, he came home to Kenosha every night. The North Shore railroad had stops at Great Lakes and Kenosha, so it was easy."[27] Ferraro was discharged from the Navy on 26 May 1919; he stayed on at Great Lakes as a civilian employee until he returned to Kenosha sometime in the early 1920s.[28] Ferraro's brother, Serafino, was also a tailor in Kenosha, and he served in the US Army during the war.

Antonio (Anthony) Spizzirri was born in 1889 and came to the United States sometime before 1913.[29] Spizzirri moved to Chicago, where he lived with his brothers, who were also tailors. Spizzirri, who ran his own tailor shop, enlisted in the Navy at Great Lakes Training Station on 25 April 1918. Spizzirri, at 5' 4.75" tall and 179 pounds, was not within Navy enlistment physical standards, but he was being recruited for his tailoring skills, and his record bears the notation: "Obesity waived for special duty as tailor."[30] Spizzirri was also enlisted as a fireman, 1st class; no doubt the increased pay made up for possible loss of income from his tailoring business.

During late summer and early fall 1918, an outbreak of influenza began to take its toll at home and abroad. Where men crowded together in military bases, influenza was certain to spread. Some time in September 1918, Spizzirri was granted liberty and went to visit his family in nearby Chicago. While there he became ill with influenza, and he was transferred to the Navy hospital at Great Lakes. While in the base hospital Spizzirri died on 29 September. Thus, his service record bears the sad

The officers and men of the American Forces in Germany (AFG) salute as the casket of Scottish-born William Reid is carried from the church service to a waiting hearse on 19 January 1922. Some mystery surrounds Reid, and there are hints that he may have actually been born in Germany.

final notation: "Pneumonia Broncho. Not in line of duty. Not due to own misconduct. Taken ill while at home on liberty. Buried Chicago, Ill. No effects." At a time when many families around the world were receiving the welcome news of the armistice and the safety of their loved ones in uniform, Spizzirri's family was left to mourn the loss of their brother.

Mariano Luigi (Louis) Bruno was born in 1888 and came to the United States in 1902 to join his father and brother—both tailors—in Chicago.[31] Soon the brothers owned a tailor shop, making the most of their opportunities in America. On 27 May 1918, Bruno went to Great Lakes Naval Training Station and enlisted in the Navy. Due to his size (5' 2.75" tall and weighing 116 pounds), Bruno also needed a physical waiver: "Underheight and underweight waived for special duty."[32] Like Ferraro and Spizzirri, Bruno enlisted as a fireman, 1st class. He worked in the Great Lakes tailor shop until his discharge on 12 February 1919, after which he returned to Chicago to resume his tailoring business.

No doubt there were many other tailors, both foreign and US born, recruited by the Navy and stationed at many bases and on many ships around the world. That some of the men so recruited were below peacetime physical standards indicates the need of the Navy for their special skills, as well as the patriotism and devotion of the men who responded.

## Show Me the Way to Go Home

The lure of returning to the land of their birth was a strong pull for some foreign-born men. It appears to have been particularly strong in states such as New York, Michigan, Minnesota, North Dakota, and Washington, which share long borders with Canada.

Prior to the war, the borders between the United States and Canada were rather porous, and people tended to move back and forth easily for work or marriage. As a result, while many Canadians working and living in the States served in the American Army, a large group also returned to Canada to enlist in their own military.

Perhaps the most-common enlistments were those of Canadian-born men returning across the border and joining the Canadian army and Britons returning home to enlist in the British forces. There was a strong movement in Polish communities to join the Polish army that was being raised in France. As a result, recruiting stations were set up in cities and counties where there were large numbers of Poles or Polish Americans. They were able to find significant numbers of recruits among the men who had been exempted from the US draft for physical problems, such as poor eyesight or other reasons.[33]

One of the training camps for the Polish army was established at Niagara-on-the-Lake, Ontario, Canada, so it was a simple matter for the men to cross the border and enlist in the Polish army. While thousands of Italians returned to Italy to join the Italian army, most Italian-born men in the United States appear to have been more interested in joining the US Army than traveling back to Italy to join King Victor Emmanuel's force.

There were several documented cases of Serbian-born men returning and enlisting in the Serbian army. Perhaps the most uncommon of all was George Truska, the Russian-born resident of Rochester, New York, who returned to Russia to join the czar's army. He was reported to have been killed while fighting on the eastern front, but his death was never confirmed.[34]

**The Slavic Legion (August–November 1918)**
On 8 August 1918, one of the most uncommon Army formations in US military history was officially activated by the War Department. By this point in the war, the Army had recognized that members of some of the "oppressed people" from the Austro-Hungarian Empire might make good soldiers to fight against that empire.

The French and Italian armies had already reached this conclusion and outfitted large numbers of Czechoslovaks to serve with them against the Germans and Austrians. Likewise, the Russians had formed a large Czech legion from prisoners of war and deserters from the Austrian army. The American Army saw that fielding Slavic Legion units in the front line across from their former countrymen might also serve to "stimulate the endemic revolutionary activity" in the enemy units.[35]

There were problems with the American version. Many of the potential recruits for the Slavic Legion were already in training camps or awaiting orders to report; indeed, some of them had been classified as "enemy aliens." The first members of the unit were to be drawn specifically from Yugoslavians, Czechs, Slovaks, and Ruthenians (Ukrainians).[36]

With this in mind, the US Army established Camp Wadsworth as the training camp for the American Slavic Legion. The Army announced that the legion "will be organized, armed and equipped as infantry regiments. Companies will, if practicable, be composed of members of the same race. . . . At present, there will be no units larger than regiments."[37] As one concession to the unusual nature of the legion, the soldiers were allowed to make out their War Risk Insurance paperwork and list beneficiaries "without restriction as to the citizenship of the allottees . . . "[38]

Ultimately, it was all for naught. When the armistice was declared, the Slavic Legion was still at Camp Wadsworth and could count only 114 enlisted men and sixteen officers on the unit rolls.

## The 26th Division Chaplains

It is not known just how many chaplains serving with the AEF were foreign born, but we might get a hint with a look at the chaplains of the 26th Division. Composed initially of National Guard units from New England, the division was nicknamed the Yankee Division. Michael Shay, in his work on the division's chaplains, provides a roster of thirty-five chaplains who served overseas with the division; thirty of them were military officers, while five others were sponsored by such organizations as the Knights of Columbus or the Jewish Welfare Board. Of the thirty-five chaplains, ten were foreign born: 1st Lt. Chauncey Adams (Canada, Congregational), 1st Lt. Israel Bettan (Lithuania, Jewish), Chaplain Osias Boucher (Canada, Catholic), 1st Lt. John DeValles (Azores, Catholic), 1st Lt. George Jonaitis (Lithuania, Catholic), 1st Lt. Anselm Mayotte (Canada, Catholic), 1st Lt. Michael Nivard (Holland, Catholic), Capt. Michael O'Connor (Ireland, Catholic), Chaplain Benjamin Riseman (Russia, Jewish), and 1st Lt. Thomas Temple (Ireland, Catholic).[39]

## The Hello Girls of the AEF

Quite possibly some of the least well-known members of the AEF were the female telephone and switchboard operators known more commonly as the "Hello Girls." The story of the "Hello Girls" began in late 1917, when Gen. Pershing's staff apprised him of the need for skilled telephone switchboard operators who could also speak French, or French-speaking ladies willing to learn the art of operating a military switchboard.

This combination was a skill set that was unavailable in the AEF because of a unique phenomenon: switchboard operators in America's rapidly growing telephone network were exclusively women. Adding to the uniqueness of the situation, the telephone switchboards in use in France were the exact type used by switchboard operators in the United States. Recognizing these factors, an "Emergency Appeal" was published in US newspapers, requesting that women with these specific skills and, importantly, a willingness to serve in France come forward to become members of the US Signal Corps.[40]

Over 2,000 women responded in the first week, and eventually the number applying reached over 7,000. Of this total, only 400 were actually accepted into the Signal Corps' program and trained. Of the 400, some seventy-two were born in foreign countries. By the end of the war there were some 223 "Hello Girls" assigned overseas to the AEF, with the rest in the States still undergoing training. After their arrival overseas, the switchboard operators were "dispersed throughout France [and] communications improved immediately."[41] In time, these women soldiers proved to be of such value that a number were decorated for bravery, and several were assigned

A group of "Hello Girls" gather in a doorway. While many of the details of their uniforms are not easily discerned, their US Army Signal Corps collar insignias are quite clear and indicate that they are full-fledged members of the Signal Corps; the formal recognition took many years to be officially resolved in their favor. *Courtesy Library of Congress*

to the Third Army to serve in the occupation of the German Rhineland, remaining until late 1919.

### A 29th Division Veteran Gets the Last Word (1990)

In the summer of 1990, a First World War veteran was interviewed by the 29th Infantry Division newsletter. The *Twenty-Niner* reported that Sicilian-born, ninety-eight-year-old John Mollica was the oldest known living 29th Infantry Division veteran.

Mollica immigrated to the United States and was working as a bricklayer in Boston when he joined the Army. After some training he was assigned to the 115th Infantry Regiment of the 29th Division. Wounded twice in combat, Mollica survived the war and returned home to New England. Surprisingly, Mollica's desire in 1990 was to be buried not in Sicily (his birthplace) or in Rhode Island (where he lived for many years), but in the Bourne National Cemetery in Massachusetts among the other soldiers. His final words on the Western Front: "It was a slaughter-house."[42]

## CHAPTER NINE

# IT'S FINALLY OVER:
## *Armistice, Occupation, and Home Again*

Two Million Doughboys reached France, most of them deficient in the basic school of the rifleman. But in the savage clinics conducted by the veteran Germans, the Doughboy progressed and by war's end he and his generals had become superior fighters.[1]

With the signing of the armistice on 11 November 1918, the AEF was going home, but in true US Army fashion, there would be delays. Under the conditions of the armistice, the US Army was required to dispatch units to serve as part of an Allied occupation force administering the German Rhineland. This force not only would serve as a buffer between Germany and the battered countries of Belgium and France but would also control the bridges across the Rhine that the German Army used to move soldiers and supplies to the Western Front during the war.

The occupation army's zones stretched in "national" layers from north to south: Belgium, Britain, United States, and France. These four zones would serve as administrative centers for receiving and inspecting war reparations material that Germany was being forced to provide to the victorious Allies. Ultimately, Pershing would dispatch eight divisions to Germany and two to Luxembourg to serve as the American contingent in the occupation.

The divisions in Germany would be under the command of the newly forming US Third Army, with headquarters in the German city of Coblenz, today known as Koblenz.

For a while it was anyone's guess which units would make up the occupation army and which units would be sent home. Equally important was knowing in what order the divisions would be returned to the States. The rumor mills were running full blast among the Doughboys in France and Belgium in the days immediately after 11 November. While many men wanted to be assigned to the Army of Occupation, probably more just wanted to go home.

Taken in Nagem, Luxembourg, during the march to the Rhine in November–December 1918, Doughboys from Section 580 of the US Army Ambulance Service are taking a break. The group includes Sgt. Eiler Lund (far left) from Denmark; Frederick A. Linthwaite (fourth from left) from Nottinghamshire, England; and Harry Kitrosser (far right) from Beltz, Russia. Kitrosser was severely wounded in July 1918 and was awarded the French *Croix de Guerre* with Bronze Star.

On 14 November, the selections became obvious when certain divisions received official orders to hand over their best draft animals to other divisions. Recognizing that the Meuse-Argonne Offensive had severely damaged the health of every unit's horses and mules, Col. George Marshall, the operational planner on the AEF staff, directed that the occupation divisions should have the best equipment and healthiest pack animals available. In spite of the age-old military practice of dumping a unit's undesirable equipment (and even personnel at times) on to another unit, some units, in particular the 29th Division, played it straight and gave up the best they had.

The commander of the 3rd Division, Maj. Gen. Robert L. Howze, later thanked the 29th for the "sportsmanlike spirit and soldierly manner in which the 29th Division had obeyed so exactly an order which afforded so great a temptation to do otherwise."[2]

Among the soldiers of the Third Army was Ernest George Northey, a twenty-six-year-old native of England. Northey had reported to Camp Funston, Kansas, on 27 April 1918 and was assigned to Company F, 314th Engineer Regiment, 89th Division. Northey later wrote that "As Engineers we were trained for fighting as well as for Engineering work." His training in "fighting" consisted of "Bayonet and Grenade course need[ed] for training of the regiment in Hand to Hand fighting." Northey also described typical engineer training: "Our Engineering work consisted of roads and trails, Bridges, and field Fortifications also mine demolition."[3] All this and more would serve Northey and his fellow engineers well in France; the 89th Division was one of the best of the National Army divisions and saw its share of combat.

After the armistice Northey marched with the 89th into Germany. As part of the US VII Corps, the 89th Division was headquartered in the German town Prum. Of occupation duty, Northey recalled: "[T]he people there sure treated us fine, couldn't be better, a lot better than the French did and we had good times there."[4] This opinion was shared by many American soldiers, who found some of the French people less than welcoming and often believed the French were price gouging the Doughboys.[5]

Also serving in the 89th was Kim Fong. Fong was born in China in 1891 and had married at the young age of fifteen. He was already a father of two young sons when he was drafted on 29 March 1918. Fong was assigned as an infantryman to Company A of the 356th Infantry Regiment. He later recalled:

Although I kept up the fight in the trenches, from start to finish, except a slight scratch on my finger, I was not injured in any way. At one time we fought with our enemies within about 200 yards, on September 12, 1918 fighting for one half day within only 50 feet. At the time of the armistice we were within only a few feet from our foes, when they raised their hands and said something which we did not understand, not until a few of them was shot down by us before we learned that they meant that the "war was over."

After serving on occupation duty in Germany, Fong returned home and was discharged on 14 June 1919. In November 1919, Fong wrote that he was "taken a vacation, intending to visit China soon."[6]

Abe Kleinberg, a twenty-eight-year-old Romanian-born Doughboy, poses for a portrait in Germany during his time with Company F, 51st Pioneer Infantry Regiment. The 51st was assigned to the US IV Corps, and Kleinberg is wearing that patch on his left shoulder. *Courtesy NYDMNA*

Often a soldier's world comes down to basics: food, clothing, shelter, and diversions. After his discharge Ernest Northey commented on some of these things. Many soldiers held the YMCA in derision because they perceived the organization charged men for candy and cigarettes when those items were supposed to be given free. There are valid arguments on both sides of this issue, but Northey had his own opinion about the civilian service organizations he encountered:

> So I have a few words to say about the YMCA which I think they weren't much good and they didn't treat the Boys right the Salvation Army was the best of all by what I seen over there also the Red Cross was good.[7]

A soldier's life could be made better or worse by such things as the competence of his leaders and the quantity and quality of his food. Of these things Northey recalled: "We also had some good officers also some bad ones. Well the food we had was rather scarce at times but we must think ourselves lucky to get what we did." Northey, who was gassed during the war, summed up his service:

> Well the Engagements I where in was at St. Michiel Sailent . . . and a good many other engagements which I must say was tough life and I don't want to see anymore of it for me although I am glad I went through and experienced what I did . . .[8]

In the meantime, the AEF HQ was busy trying to determine how to get the remainder

Pvt. 1st Class Ernest G. Northey, a twenty-six-year-old native of England and a member of Company F, 314th Engineer Regiment, 89th Division. Note that for the portrait taken after his discharge, Northey has chosen to wear a campaign hat while carefully posing so that his overseas stripes and Honorable Discharge stripe are visible. *Courtesy New Mexico, World War I, 1917–1919*

of the AEF back to the States as quickly and economically as possible. In effect, they were now dealing with three separate forces: the Third Army in Germany, the large forces in the Services of Supply that would be required to sustain the forces in France and load them onto homebound ships, and all the remaining combat divisions still in France.

Pvts. Elvero Signori, Giuseppe Galante, and Donadi pause in their occupation duties to pose for this portrait in Germany. All three were born in Italy and were assigned to Company F of the 51st Pioneer Infantry Regiment. *Courtesy NYDMNA*

One after another, the divisions that had fought in the Meuse-Argonne or had supported the British Offensive moved to training areas in central France to begin the process of reequipping. Lightly wounded men returned to their units, and attempts were made to issue new clothing and equipment to replace items that had been damaged or destroyed in the fighting. With a few exceptions, it became obvious that most of the Doughboys were going to have to endure the European winter before it would be their turn to go home. Being good soldiers, most units made an attempt to ignore the rain, sleet, and snow while performing endless drills. The more astute among them did see the "irony in maneuvers against [a pretend] enemy, after having met successfully in battle an actual enemy."[9] The 29th Division staff, realizing that they would remain in France for the foreseeable future, began to work on the three things they thought would keep the division disciplined and content: "interesting work, comfortable quarters and healthful amusements."[10]

In addition to sporting events and maneuvers, the soldiers of the AEF were given their first opportunity to be tourists. Among the favored sites to visit were Aix-les-Bains, Grenoble, and Nice. Many other soldiers were able to earn slots at French or British colleges and began studies in programs they could never have afforded back home. Others were quick to take advantage of the facilities and activities offered by various American welfare agencies: the Red Cross, YMCA, Salvation Army, Knights of Columbus, and the Jewish Welfare League. The YMCA established huts in the divisional training areas, and the Doughboys who visited them were given the opportunity to occasionally converse with one of the female canteen workers. As the 29th's history reported, "While there may be conflicting opinions as to the advisability of having sent woman workers to France . . . it will be difficult to find any member of the 29th Division who has anything but words of praise and gratitude to them for the very real help and the many hours of companionship they provided."[11]

In spite of all the efforts to keep them busy and productive, the Doughboys were impatient to return home. The homesickness was so pervasive that the standard Doughboy question since the Mexican border campaign of "When do we eat?" had changed to "When are we going home?"[12]

Perhaps of comfort to the Doughboys awaiting their turn to go home was the knowledge that President Wilson was also in France with them. Although his focus clearly remained on his attempts to create the League of Nations, he did find time to visit some of the units of his army. Wilson paid a visit to the 26th Division on Christmas Day and reviewed some of the units before stopping to have lunch with the new division commander, Maj. Gen. Harry C. Hale, and his staff.[13]

By this time the 26th had settled into the 8th Training Area near Montigny-le-Roi. After lunch the president traveled to an area near Langres, where another group of Doughboys awaited his inspection. Over 10,000 soldiers representing the 6th, 26th, 77th, 80th, and 82nd Divisions were reviewed by Wilson before he returned to Paris to continue his struggle to achieve an honorable peace. Ultimately, the Doughboys were more successful in their war efforts than Wilson was in his peace efforts, but that disappointment lay in the future. At the end of 1918, most Doughboys were optimistic that the future was bright and that they would go home soon.

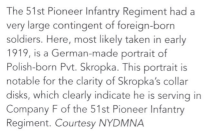

The 51st Pioneer Infantry Regiment had a very large contingent of foreign-born soldiers. Here, most likely taken in early 1919, is a German-made portrait of Polish-born Pvt. Skropka. This portrait is notable for the clarity of Skropka's collar disks, which clearly indicate he is serving in Company F of the 51st Pioneer Infantry Regiment. *Courtesy NYDMNA*

Pvt. Alessio Marchesi (right), a thirty-one-year-old native of Italy, served with the 117th Engineer Regiment, 42nd Division. Marchesi served in the Champagne front, on the Marne, at St. Mihiel, and in the Meuse Argonne Offensive. He also served in the Army of Occupation in Germany for five months. *Courtesy New Mexico, World War I Records, 1917–1919*

The Doughboys' hope for a speedy return to the United States soon evaporated. In spite of the massive efforts on their behalf, it was going to take time for the Navy and the fleet of converted warships, cargo ships, and passenger ships to take them all home. The 91st Division traveled by train from Le Mans to St. Nazaire in the middle of March 1919; by early April the entire division had left France. The 26th Division began sailing in late April 1919. The 79th was a month after that. The 88th would not begin their journey home from their training area near Le Mans until the middle of May.

In contrast to the combat divisions, those divisions that had been broken apart to serve as a source of replacements or as depot divisions received another unpleasant surprise. They were to be at the mercy of the transportation schedulers, and their depleted, skeletonized units would be transported as they could be fit into the schedule. In the case of the 86th Division, its first units sailed on 3 January 1919, but it was not until 2 July that the last of the 86th Division arrived on the East Coast and headed for their demobilization at Camp Grant.[14] The story was much the same for the other replacement or depot divisions, such as the 34th, 38th, 76th, 83rd, and 85th. The AEF staff attempted to get the skeletonized divisions out of the way quickly, but because the goal was to move as many troops as quickly as possible and to load the vessels fully, the smaller units were often bumped out of line.

After the cold, wet winter ended and the advent of spring, the Doughboys realized the time was finally drawing near for their departure from France. Each week, men could read the list of departing units and knew that sometime soon it would be their turn to go.

There was one more major event in the life of each combat division before it was allowed to leave France. In keeping with his tradition of personally decorating and thanking the units of the AEF prior to their departure, Gen. Pershing visited as many of the departing units as he could. Rain or shine, Pershing conducted an inspection in ranks of assembled units and attempted to make eye contact with every soldier. After the inspection, the AEF commander would decorate the regimental and division flags. With the division and regimental commanders by his side, Pershing also presented a number of individual medals to deserving soldiers. When the last medal had been presented, the unit would pass in review for Pershing and the senior staff. If time allowed, the AEF commander would call the men to come forward and gather around him so he could thank them for their service.[15]

It was a busy time for Pershing, but he was aware of the esteem with which the Doughboys held him. In return, he wanted them to feel personally thanked for their sacrifices and service. Secretary of War Newton Baker joined Pershing in Europe in April 1919 and was able to participate in a number of the farewell formations, including the ceremony at Trier, Germany, for the 89th Division and at Gondrecourt, France, for the 88th Division.

As each unit received its notification to report to the port, there was an increased emphasis on delousing the entire division to ensure that no "cooties" made it on the ships going home. After that, it was a short journey via the French railcars that the AEF had come to refer to as "side door Pullmans" to the seaports.

Boarding many of the same ships that had carried them to Europe, the Doughboys once again set sail on the Atlantic. Without having to zigzag or travel in convoys for fear of submarine attacks, the ships traveled more quickly and sailed on a direct course to their East Coast destinations, reaching them usually in a little over a week. In typical troop ship fashion, the entire day was seemingly spent waiting in the chow line.

Pvt. 1st Class Kim Fong, born in China in 1891, and married at age fifteen, was already the father of two young sons when he was drafted in March 1918. Fong was assigned to the 356th Infantry Regiment, 89th Division. He served with the unit in France and later in the occupation of Germany. Fong is wearing the 89th Division patch on his shoulder and has the smaller version Third Army patch sewn just above his two overseas stripes. *Courtesy Utah Military Records, 1861-1970*

For the troops arriving in Newport News, such as the 29th and 80th Divisions, there was usually a march through the recently built "Victory Arch" in the port. From there they marched to nearby Camp Stuart for final processing, or movement to another demobilization site.

Other divisions, such as the 27th, 28th, 78th, 79th, 88th, and 91st, disembarked at the ports in the New York City area. After short stays at Camp Mills, Camp Merritt, or Camp Upton, they moved on to their demobilization sites: the 28th to Camp Dix, the 78th and 79th to Camp Meade and Camp Dix, the 88th to Camp Dodge, and the 91st all the way to Camp Lewis, on the West Coast. And the story was much the same for the other returning divisions. By now the National Army and National Guard divisions contained men from many different locations. With combat losses, and for many divisions a heavy influx of replacements, whatever local character a division may have had in 1917 was gone by the end of 1918. With this in mind, each division, upon returning to such reception centers as Camp Mills or Camp Upton, formed detachments of men from various regions and sent them to a camp in that area for discharge. For example, groups of men who entered service from Illinois, Wisconsin, and Iowa were sent to Camp Grant for final discharge. Aside from this sensible provision, the Army followed Army Chief of Staff Peyton March's guidance that the soldiers were to be discharged by units, not by individuals. Also in accordance with March's wishes, the divisions, after the various discharge detachments were sent on their way, moved to demobilization stations closest to where the majority of the men had entered service.[16]

Born in 1895 near Palermo, Sicily, Charles Chiara came to the States in 1902 and settled in Harrisburg, Pennsylvania. In July 1917, Chiara enlisted in the Pennsylvania National Guard. Chiara's unit was later reorganized as Company C, 103rd Ammunition Train, 28th Division. Chiara later attributed divine protection for keeping him safe through the Champagne-Marne Defensive, Aisne-Marne Offensive, Fisme sector, Oise-Aisne Offensive, and the Meuse-Argonne Offensive without a scratch. *Courtesy Pennsylvania Archives, Ancestry.com®*

All this had the effect of sending men, whatever their division of assignment, to a camp near their home of record for discharge. Once all inspections and equipment turn-in was completed, they were ready to be discharged. They would then draw their final pay and railroad fare to return home. Each soldier was allowed to retain a full set of uniforms, gas mask, and helmet. This was in accordance with guidance from Gen. March that every soldier was to be given "a uniform, shoes,

A small portion of a larger unit photograph of the 49th Infantry Regiment Supply Company. The 49th was formed in Syracuse, New York, and attached to the 83rd Division in France. On the back of the photo, the original owner has numbered and listed the name of each soldier, along with comments: the two men in the second row, from the left, are labeled as Welch (Irish) and Moskowitz (Jewish). Behind them are Barardi, Levinoff, and Jelenski. Other names on the photo also give an idea of the international flavor of this company: Saurwein, Solak, Bonkowski, Rakosky, Vittaro, Cabella, and Baryoletti.

and an overcoat or raincoat. In the case of overseas men, helmets and gas masks were issued as souvenirs."[17] After a final inspection and company formation the Doughboys were released from active duty and went home.

Part of the Army still remained in Germany, occupying the American sector of the Rhineland. Its name had changed from the US Third Army to the American Forces in Germany (AFG), but the job and shoulder patch remained the same.

Over time, and under the firm but fair leadership of Maj. Gen. Henry T. Allen, the AFG would become known as the most elite unit in the US Army. Comprising combat veterans and new recruits, the AFG would remain as the American military presence in Europe until 1923. Many men who eagerly enlisted before or soon after the United States entered the war were assigned to Regular Army units that, much to the recruits' chagrin, remained stateside during the war. Some of them were given the opportunity to go overseas as part of the Army of Occupation.

One such man was Salvatore Rucchetto, who was born in Italy in December 1899. Rucchetto came to the United States as a young child in 1903. He was living in Indiana when, under the name Salvatore Rockette (sometimes spelled "Rockett"), he enlisted in the Army on 19 January 1917. This was three months before the United States entered the war and one month after his seventeenth birthday.

The model M1917 service coat belonging to Sgt./Bugler Nieves Reynosa. Born in Chihuahua, Mexico, Reynosa enlisted in the US Army in 1916, and served in France with the 39th Infantry Regiment, 4th Division. He earned four campaign clasps for his Victory Medal: Aisne-Marne, St. Mihiel, Meuse-Argonne, and the Defensive Sector. *Courtesy of Rogier van de Hoef*

Rockette was assigned to Headquarters Company, 50th Infantry Regiment. The 50th was a new Regular Army regiment made up of men from other regiments bolstered with recruits and, later, draftees. On 28 October 1917, the regiment moved to Camp Greene, North Carolina, to begin training for overseas deployment. Soon the regiment was ordered to perform guard duty in the mid-Atlantic coastal states, relieving National Guard troops who had been performing this anti-sabotage duty. In August, the various elements of the regiment began congregating at Camp Sevier to become part of the newly forming 20th Division.

Rockette remained stateside until at least 4 November 1918, when he became a US citizen at Camp Sevier. On his naturalization document Rockette gave his birth date as 1 December 1898; no doubt this was the date he used when he enlisted, since he had lied about his age to appear to be eighteen years old at the time of enlistment. The war ended before the 50th could go overseas. Rockette remained in the Army and was sent overseas as part of what was originally known as the "Silesian Brigade," a force intended to serve as peacekeepers during the Silesian Plebiscite to determine the border demarcation between German and Poland.

Shortly after the 50th's arrival in Coblenz, the US government discontinued that mission and reassigned the regiment to the AFG. On 27 January 1920, Rockette, by now a private 1st class, reenlisted at Coblenz, Germany.

In March 1921, Rockette returned to the United States. He was sent to Fort Slocum, New York, where he was discharged from the Army on 18 March. After his return to Indiana, Rockette must have greatly missed the Army; on 8 June, almost three months after his discharge, he journeyed to Fort Sheridan to reenlist in the Army.[18]

With the departure of the AFG from its duty in the German Rhineland in February 1923, the last of the Doughboys had left Europe. Remaining behind now in Europe were the dead and a few soldiers working diligently, still trying to send home the remains of the deceased soldiers that had been requested by their families. Unfortunately, even this last solemn duty would be complicated by the complexities of the names of the deceased, as well as the native tongues of grieving family members. As will be seen in the next chapter, it would be several years before some mourning families would achieve closure. Others never would.

Pvt. Alfredo Scastilla survived the war, only to die of lobar pneumonia while serving in the occupation of Luxembourg. Born in Amagne, Italy, Scastilla served in Battery D, 21st Field Artillery, 5th Division. Making his sacrifice even more poignant, the Army misspelled his name Scastella on his headstone in Walferdange cemetery just north of Luxembourg City.

Salvatore Calanni (standing), an Italian-born Doughboy, was originally trained as a mechanic in the Air Service but was later assigned to the 104th Engineer Regiment, 29th Division, and served under the name Sam Calan. In this informal picture Calanni has made sure his service coat is open to show his battlefield souvenir German Army belt and buckle. *Courtesy Calanni family and Virginia National Guard*

The Model M1917 helmet brought home by Sam Calanni after his service in the 29th Division was completed. Calanni's family recounts that Sam was immensely proud of his service in the Army and at least into the 1960s was still using his US Army issue shaving kit. *Courtesy Calanni family and Virginia National Guard*

Shown here are the gas mask carrier and dog tags belonging to Sam Calanni. Note that in addition to painting the 29th Division symbol on the carrier, Calanni added his two overseas stripes, his unit name, and the name of 29th Division Commander Gen. (Charles) Morton. *Courtesy Calanni family and Virginia National Guard*

First Sgt. Henry A. Johnson, Company E, 28th Infantry Regiment, 1st Division, shown with his wife. Johnson was born in Sweden in 1890, and came to the United States in 1907. He enlisted in the 28th in 1915, and served with the unit through all its battles and the Army of Occupation. In addition to his victory medal, he is wearing a Mexican Campaign ribbon, a marksman badge, and a French *Fourragere*. *Courtesy 1st Division Museum at Cantigny*

Frederick Bosenberg (right) was born in Hanover, Germany. Inducted into the Army in June 1918, Bosenberg was originally assigned to the 49th Engineer Battalion, a railway maintenance unit. After the armistice he was assigned to the Inter-Allied Railway Commission in Coblenz.

Canadian-born Fenwick Dorman was attending forestry school at the University of Montana and working as a topographic draftsman and surveyor when he entered the Army on 25 February 1918. Dorman was assigned to the 29th Engineer Regiment, a mapping and topographical unit that was stationed throughout France. By October 1918, combat had taken a toll on Dorman, and he later listed his service connected ailments as "Gas, Enfluenza, Pneumonia, Pulmonary Tuberculosis." On 4 November 1918, Pvt. Dorman was discharged with 100 percent temporary disability. *Courtesy New Mexico, World War I Records, 1917–1919*

Born in Holland, Capt. Albert E. Haan served in the US Army prior to the war. He joined the Michigan National Guard shortly thereafter and maintained his military ties. In this picture taken in Paris on Christmas Day in 1918, the captain poses with his crutch and a heavily bandaged foot. Haan remained on duty while rehabilitating until 1920. *Courtesy Brennan C. Gauthier*

A group of soldiers from Battery F, 6th Field Artillery Regiment, pose together for a portrait, ca. 1920. On the left is Pvt. van der Meer, a Dutch-born soldier. Under magnification it can be seen that van der Meer is wearing an artillery disk with felt backing on his left collar, and he is wearing the older model service coat with external pockets, while the other two soldiers have the M1918 model coat with hidden pockets.

Another Italian-born pioneer infantryman Antonio Visione. In this postwar portrait, Visione is wearing the 3rd Army patch. This would tentatively identify him as being assigned to one of the pioneer infantry regiments that were stationed in the Coblenz region with the Third Army headquarters. *Courtesy of Brennan C. Gauthier*

Mess Sgt. Banni G. Pankevich was born in Russia in 1892, and was serving in the 3rd Division, on the west side of the Rhine, when he sent this photograph of his unit kitchen to a friend. On the back, in broken but understandable Russian, Pankevich wrote, "Dear friend, sent you my picture. There are my cooks and my kitchen. One year I'm in war, thinking to come to America soon, if God give to be healthy." Pankevich, seated in the center by the stove, remained in the Army until June 1920.

Soldiers from the 16th Infantry Regiment, 1st Division, stand in formation after receiving Distinguished Service Crosses in Mertert, Luxembourg, in November 1918. Cpl. Mieczyslaw Brocki (far left), alternatively listed as being born either in Poland or in Chicago, was a two-time DSC recipient, the first for capturing two machine guns at Soissons and the second for leading his platoon to safety after personally killing six Germans while using his rifle as a club. Russian-born Pvt. Emanuel Karch (far right) received his award for heroism while capturing two German machine guns at Soissons on 21 July 1918. *Courtesy 1st Division Museum at Cantigny*

A ceramic souvenir plate belonging to Swedish-born Erland Holtz. Holtz, a veteran of the Spanish-American War, served with the 2nd Field Signal Battalion, 1st Division, during the occupation of the Rhineland and made sure that the local artisan carefully painted all of Holtz's campaigns on the inside bowl of the plate.

The armistice meant very little to John J. Byrne, a Doughboy from Dublin, Ireland. Byrne was serving in the 339th Infantry Regiment and deployed to be part of the US Army contingent in the northern Russia campaign. While the rest of the United States was celebrating the armistice, Byrne and his comrades were fighting for their lives against the Red Army in the Battle of Toulgas. The 339th did not return to the States until late 1919. *Courtesy Rochester and Monroe County, NY*

Italian-born Antonio Montemanaro (left) poses with two of his friends at a German photo studio in Coblenz during the occupation. Montemanaro had served as an artilleryman in the 321st Field Artillery Regiment, 82nd Division, during the war and was assigned to the 2nd Battalion, 6th Field Artillery Regiment.

Demitri Petroff, a Bulgarian-born Doughboy, also served in the postwar Army of Occupation. In this studio portrait, Petroff is wearing a medical corps collar disk with a felt background. *Courtesy of Brennan C. Gauthier*

Among the soldiers serving in the occupation were a number of German-born Doughboys. Seen here (far right) is Cpl. Curtis R. Birkholz, born in Berlin, Germany, in 1897. Posing with him are his fellow 3rd Pioneer Infantry Regiment NCOs Sgt. Edmund C. Ebert and Cpl. Frank Kowalski. *Courtesy Chuck Thomas Collection*

Cpl. Salvatore Rockette (Rucchetto, left) with Cpls. Huarrett and Taylor, 50th Infantry Regiment. "Taken in Mayen, Germany, Sept. 19, 1920. Serving in Army of Occupation." Rockette was born in Italy in 1899. *Courtesy of Gemma Rocchette*

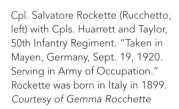

Among the soldiers serving in the AFG was Czechoslovakian-born Joseph Vomacka, seen here with his wife. Vomacka appears to have served in the Army for quite a while, on the basis of the five service stripes on his left cuff. The fact he is not wearing any overseas stripes on his model M1918 service coat would indicate he was not assigned to the AFG until sometime between 1920 and 1922.

## CHAPTER TEN

# INTO THE LAND OF
# MY DREAMS

Well I would say a lot more about the war but its no use saying all we know. . . . I hope never to see another war.[1]

The end of the war brought joy to millions of families around the world; for them, the news that their loved ones in uniform would soon be coming home warmed their hearts and gladdened their spirits. Having passed through the double danger of war and Spanish flu pandemic, they were comforted in their belief that 1919 would ring in a period of peace. Many also truly believed that the service of foreign-born soldiers, as well as first-generation Americans, would remove the hyphen that labeled an individual as an "Italian-American," a "Greek-American," a "Polish-American," etc., and all would now be simply "Americans." Like keeping the world "safe for democracy," this hope would also be dashed in the harsh light of the 1920s. Nevertheless, it was an optimistic group of soldiers who survived the war and the flu to return home to their families.

Other families continued to mourn the passing of loved ones. The war's end brought a new level of grief to their life, as they now had to deal with the final disposition of their loved one's remains. Many American soldiers had family, and even next of kin, still residing in Europe. For them a level of poignancy added to their grief. The story of one such incident serves to indicate what must have been a trying ordeal for many families. It also shows the struggle with spelling "foreign" names and addresses that bedeviled War Department clerks throughout the war.

Eugenio Scarloto was born in Italy in 1889, came to the United States in 1906, and settled in Kenosha, Wisconsin.[2] He was drafted and reported for duty in March 1918, was sent to Camp Custer, Michigan, and was assigned to the 2nd Battalion, 160th Depot Brigade. On his enlistment documents Scarloto listed his uncle, Salvatore

Scarloto, with whom he had lived in Kenosha, as his next of kin; this small detail would have a significant impact later. Scarloto was sent to Camp Gordon, where he became part of the 11th Company, 1st Replacement Regiment, destined to become a replacement for an overseas unit. On 30 June, he sailed for France. On arrival Scarloto was assigned to the 164th Infantry Regiment, 41st Division, a replacement unit sending men to fill vacancies in combat divisions at the front.

Shortly after his arrival in France, Scarloto underwent further training and was sent to the 23rd Infantry Regiment, 2nd Division. The 2nd Division was a Regular Army division with an infantry complement consisting of one brigade of two Army regiments and one brigade of two Marine Corps regiments. It would be rated as one of the best divisions—probably among the top three—in the AEF.

Scarloto received still more training from the combat veterans in the 23rd Infantry Regiment. He participated in the St. Mihiel Offensive from 12–16 September, after which the 2nd Division participated in the Battle of Blanc Mont in early October. From there the division was dispatched to participate in the ongoing Meuse-Argonne Offensive. From 1–11 November, the 23rd Infantry Regiment attacked German positions near the Meuse River. At some point, either during the Blanc Mont action or during the subsequent fighting along the Meuse River, Scarloto was wounded.

He was eventually sent to Evacuation Hospital 19, where he died on 19 November 1918, eight days after the war ended. He was buried the next day in AEF Cemetery #84 near Allerey, Saone-et-Loire, France. The Grave Location Blank completed by Chaplain J. D. Ascham initially gave his name as Scarleto but was then corrected to Scarloto. His cause of death was reported as "G.S.W.," or gunshot wound. One identity disk was interred with Scarloto's body, while the other was nailed to a peg marking his grave. Showing how easily information could become confused, the next of kin is listed as Sybato Scarleto. It is not too difficult to imagine that a company clerk asking Eugenio this information might misunderstand his Italian accent and write "Sybato" instead of Salvatore.

At some point Salvatore Scarloto was notified of his nephew's death. At this time, the options for the next of kin included having the remains buried in an American cemetery in France, returning the remains to the United States for interment in a national cemetery, or returning the remains to the next of kin for interment in a cemetery of the next of kin's choice. Salvatore, as the declared next of kin, filled out a card indicating he wanted Eugenio's remains to be sent to him in Kenosha.

On 26 March 1919, a Quartermaster Corps official completed a Graves Registration Service form for use in keeping track of remains. The form has Eugenio's given name correctly spelled but also bears a handwritten "correction" to the name, spelling it "Eugenic." By June 1920, as the US government was preparing the final disposition of all servicemen's remains, there appeared to be no change, since Salvatore apparently still wanted his nephew's remains to be shipped to him in Kenosha. Forms filled out at this time still show "Eugenic" as the given name.

On 21 July 1920, the Graves Registration Service wrote to Salvatore, asking by way of final confirmation if he still desired Eugenio's remains to be sent to him in

Posing with Director of Citizenship at the Bureau of Naturalization Raymond Crist, this group is a good representation of the many different homelands from which soldiers came. Judging by the presence or absence of overseas service chevrons on their uniforms, they also represent a good mixture of soldiers who served in France, as well as those who remained in the States. *Courtesy Library of Congress*

Kenosha. By this time Salvatore had changed his mind, as his handwritten letter of correction to Chief of the Cemeterial Division Maj. Charles C. Pierce reveals:

> Dear Sir,
>
> I Salvatore Scarloto, the nearest relative of the deceased Pvt. soldier Eugenio Scarloto I wish to have his body to remain in France and I also wish to have the right name of his grave and the location of the cemetry.

The letter from the Graves Registration Service once again spelled Eugenio's given name incorrectly. Salvatore desired that the War Department get the name correct for the gravestone; he also wrote that Eugenio's father and mother were Gabriele and Gelsomina Scarloto, and that Eugenio had two brothers, Achille and Gioacchino, and one sister, Concetta.

As noted earlier, on entering the Army, Scarloto had declared that his uncle Salvatore was his next of kin. Now, with this new information, it became apparent to the War Department that Scarloto had closer living relatives. On 5 August, Maj. Pierce requested that Salvatore "furnish this office with address of Gabriele Scarloto,

For this reunion the town of Chisholm, Minnesota, has gathered their Slovenian veterans for a welcome-home party and group portrait. While it appears that most of the men in this picture remained in the States during the war, the sergeant (front row far left) appears to have spent some eighteen months overseas, and the star above his overseas stripes indicates he was among the first Doughboys to go to France.

father of the late Private Eugenie Scarloto [note the continued incorrect spelling of "Eugenio"]." On 16 August Salvatore responded:

Dear Sir,

In replay of your august 5th 20 wich I will wright the corret address of Gabriele Scarloto his Signor Gabriele Scarloto di Gioacchino, Ufficio Postale, Cosenza, Province Cosenza, Italy.

With this latest information, the War Department sent a letter to Gabriele Scarloto on 24 August; the letter was improperly addressed thus:

Signor Gabriele Scarlotte,

G' Gioacchino, Uficio Portate,

Corenga, Province of Corenga,

Italy

In this letter, the War Department basically gave Gabriele the same options as to the disposition of Eugenio's remains as it had to Salvatore. The letter further stipulates that if Gabriele desired to have the remains shipped to Italy:

such transfer will be subject to the health regulations and sanitation laws for France and Italy, and should the operation of such instrumentalities prevent the removal of the body in the manner desired, it will remain in the care and custody of the American Graves Registration Service in Europe and will be cared for under the supervision of this Government.

The letter concluded with the department's wish "to convey to you its assurance of sympathy in your bereavement." One suspects that, with Italy's long experience of handling large amounts of transatlantic mail, some of which must have been curiously addressed, such an address would not have posed a serious obstacle to delivery. That said, it is not clear the letter ever reached Gabriele. What is known is that by 30 September 1920, the decision was reached to keep Eugenio Scarloto's remains in France.

Accordingly, the remains were exhumed from the cemetery at Allerey, and the disinterment report stated that Scarloto was "buried in uniform, and in wooden box. Badly decomposed, recognition impossible." No identification tag was found on the body, but the tag on the grave marker was still there. A general description followed: "No effects found. Post mortem on head. Such bodies as were identified in this row checked out under proper crosses." By an examination of the body it was impossible to determine height and weight. His hair color was "apparently dark brown" and it was "abundant" and "straight." On 20 June 1922, Scarloto was finally reburied in

## UNITED·STATES·ARMY·

### IN MEMORY OF

*Private First Class Izzy Scheinbaum, Co H. 147th Infantry*
*who died October 30th 1918*
He bravely laid down his life for the cause of his country.
His name will ever remain fresh in the hearts of his friends
and comrades. The record of his honorable service will be
preserved in the archives of the American Expeditionary Forces.

*John J. Pershing*
Commander-in-chief

The commemoration certificate issued by the AEF in honor of Russian-born Pvt. 1st Class Izzie Scheinbaum, who was residing in Cleveland, Ohio, when he registered for the draft. Scheinbaum had been a "declarant" immigrant intending to become a US citizen and was serving in the 147th Infantry Regiment, 37th Division, when he was killed in action near Cruyshautem, Belgium, on 30 October 1918.

grave 21, row 7, block A at the St. Mihiel American Cemetery, Thiaucourt, France. To the last, his name was being misspelled on official forms. A correction was made in the late 1920s, and his gravestone now bears his correct name.

Scarloto's final burial did not "close the books" on his case. On 21 November 1924, his entitlement to the Wisconsin veterans' bonus of fifty dollars was canceled because no one was prosecuting the claim.

Later, in 1929, the government began planning to send the mothers of fallen soldiers on a pilgrimage to France to visit grave sites. The War Department, still unable to contact any Scarloto family members in Italy, wrote again to Salvatore in Kenosha, asking for Gelsomina Scarloto's address. Salvatore now provided the address "Sig. Scarloto Gelsomina, Prov. Cosenza, Via Pietraro, Ferma Posta Italia." In response to a query of whether or not Gelsomina would like to attend the pilgrimage, Salvatore (or another relative) wrote, "We don't know, write to her." It is not known if Gelsomina was ever contacted about the pilgrimage or if she attended. Finally, on 3 March 1933, there is an annotation on a government claims card stating that Scarloto was twenty-nine years old and single at the time of his enlistment, and that there was "no record of any loco" (referring probably to the fact that no one other than his mother had served as a "parent" to Scarloto during his minority).

With that, Scarloto's case was closed; a foreign-born Doughboy had served his adopted country in time of war and had given his life in a distant land, and there he will repose for eternity.

A similar case also involving an Italian immigrant soldier serves to illustrate the vexing problem of trying to correspond with relatives in English and Italian in two different countries while coordinating with several government agencies also in two different countries.

Luigi Perri was born in Italy and was living in Chicago when he entered military service in 1917. On his enlistment paperwork he claimed his brother, Michael Perri of Chicago, as next of kin. Luigi was eventually assigned to the 132nd Infantry Regiment, 33rd Division.[3] The 33rd was originally made up of Illinois National Guard units that had been activated in the months immediately following the US declaration of war. During its training period at Camp Logan, Texas, the 33rd was infused with a large number of draftees from the various camps around the country, and most likely joining them at this time was Pvt. Luigi Perri.

The 33rd Division went to France in May 1918; by 21 June, the 132nd Infantry Regiment underwent training from British forces. On 4 July, well before completion of their training, Companies A and G, 132nd Infantry Regiment, were loaned to the 4th Australian Infantry Brigade to take part in an attack at Hamel and Vaire Woods. When the Australian rolling barrage started, it fell short, landing among the Americans as they formed for the attack. This caused a number of casualties, and among them was Pvt. Luigi Perri.[4]

On 5 July, the 132nd's regimental chaplain, 1st Lt. John L. O'Donnell, buried Perri close to where he fell in Bayonvillers, near Vaire Woods. According to O'Donnell, one of Perri's identification tags was buried with his body, and the other was affixed to the British grave peg used to mark the grave. It is uncertain when Perri's body was next moved, but on 12 June 1919, Australian soldiers disinterred his body from Vaire Woods British Military Cemetery and reinterred it in grave 10, row A, plot 5 at Crucifix Corner British Military Cemetery. At the time, the Australians reported no identification tag on the body and no other means of identification found.

After the war, the War Department wrote to Michael Perri in Chicago, requesting to know his wishes regarding the disposition of Luigi's remains. Perri replied that he wanted his brother's remains to be sent to him in Chicago for private reburial. Then, in August 1920, the War Department sent Michael Perri G.R.S. Form #120, Shipping Inquiry, for him to make a formal request for the body of his deceased brother. On this form Michael Perri stated that he was the nearest living relative of Luigi Perri and that he desired the body to be shipped to him in Chicago.

On this form Michael Perri also indicated that while both of Luigi's parents were dead, he had an older brother, Giovanni Perri, living in Italy, as well as two other brothers in the United States and another brother and sister in Italy. Thus, according to the rules in force, it was the older brother, Giovanni Perri, who was actually Luigi Perri's next of kin. It should therefore be Giovanni who determined the disposition of Luigi's remains.

With this new information, Maj. Charles C. Pierce of the Quartermaster General's office, Graves Registration Service (the same man who corresponded with Eugenio Scarloto's family), wrote to Michael Perri on 24 August 1920:

[Y]ou are informed that before this office can comply with your wishes [to have Luigi Perri's body shipped to Michael in Chicago], it is necessary that you obtain a signed statement from the oldest brother [Giovanni Perri] of the late soldier, showing his consent to this action, and forward same to this office with the least possible delay.

On 30 August, Michael wrote to Maj. Pierce. Citing Pierce's letter, Michael stated:

I have noted what you say with reference to obtaining a signed statement from the oldest brother. My oldest brother is in Europe at the present time and I will have considerable difficulty in locating him, if indeed I am able to locate him, however if the arrangement can only be made by securing a signed statement from my oldest brother will you please advise if this consent by him should be procured on some particular form and if so will you kindly send to me such form for use in procuring said statement.

Pierce wrote back to Michael on 13 September, reiterating the necessity for a statement from the oldest brother, and then continuing:

It is therefore requested that you make further efforts to locate your brother and obtain from him a written statement . . . that he has no objection to the removal of the body to the United States for delivery to you. The statement requires no special form. Your early attention to this matter will be greatly appreciated.

While all this correspondence was going on, other letters flew between government agencies concerning the same issue. In that long-ago, pre-email age, copies, carbons, file numbers, and cross references were multiplied with abandon. On 5 November, Pierce wrote to the American Graves Registration Service in Europe:

It is requested that you communicate with the following relative, comply with desires so obtained and initiate Form #114 in case the same is necessary:

Mr. Giovanni Perri (Brother), Castrolibero, Italy.

Clearly in an effort to resolve the issue as quickly as possible, Pierce was trying to approach the matter on two different fronts. This would cause unfortunate complications.

In the meantime, Michael Perri had secured a statement of consent from his brother Giovanni in Italy. On 24 November, Michael wrote to Maj. Pierce:

As requested by you, I have secured the consent of my oldest brother, Giovanni Perri, to return the body and I am enclosing his letter herewith. Would be glad to have arrangements made as promptly as possible for return of the body to me at 729 DeKoven Street, Chicago, Illinois.

Giovanni Perri's statement, written in English, was direct and simple:

Dear Brother:

This letter is for the purpose of advising you that I consent to having the remains of our brother, Private Luigi Perri, returned to the United States, and body turned over to you for burial in the United States.

On 21 December, Pierce wrote to the American Graves Registration Service in Europe, advising them that Luigi Perri's relatives desired that his body be returned to the United States. It would seem that everything was in order for the shipment of Perri's remains to Chicago. But Michael Perri had not heard anything from the War Department since he sent his brother's consent statement in November. On 15 January 1921, Michael again wrote to Maj. Pierce. After quoting his (Michael's) letter of 24 November, Michael concluded: "I would be glad to have you advise me the status of this matter. Will you kindly do so?"

While all this was going on, Luigi Perri's body was disinterred on 22 January 1921. The body was "in blanket, in pine box, badly decomposed." The workers reported no identification tags on Perri's body or on the grave marker. However, a "reburial paper found on body in bottle reads 'Pvt. Luigi Perri, 1391161, Co. G, 132 Inf.' Collar ornament found on body marked 'G-132.'" The state of decomposition of the body made it impossible to determine Perri's height or weight, and there was no hair left on the skull. The severity of Perri's fatal wound is evident in the workers' remarks concerning marks of wounds received at the time of casualty: "Left pelvis, left shoulder blade missing. Lower third of right fibula and upper jaw fractured. Lower jaw missing." In addition, almost all his upper teeth were missing. Clearly Perri had suffered a devastating wound from the artillery fire. The exhumation form still indicated that the body was to be shipped to Michael Perri in Chicago.

On 31 January, still not having heard from the War Department, Michael Perri again wrote to Maj. Pierce. Perri cited his letters of 24 November and 15 January and requested an update on the matter:

May I not receive a reply at once as there has been a considerable lapse of time now since my letter of November 24th to you requesting arrangements be made for return of the body.

On 2 February, the Chief of the American Graves Registration Service in Europe approved release of Perri's body for shipment to the port and further shipment to its final destination. Finally, on 4 February, Capt. R. E. Shannon of the Quartermaster Corps wrote to Michael with the welcome news that his brother's body was to be shipped to him:

> You are advised that your request to have the remains returned to the United States and shipped to you . . .will be complied with. It is regretted that definite information cannot be given as to the date of return. . . . The Department desires to convey to you renewed assurance of its sympathy in your bereavement.

As a result of Maj. Pierce's letter to the American Graves Registration Service in Europe back in November, Luigi's oldest brother, Giovanni, completed an affidavit in Italy requesting that Luigi's body be returned to him in Italy and not sent to Chicago. The statement, completed on 13 March in Italian and translated into English, was witnessed by Benedetto Veme, mayor of Castrolibero. In addition to formal legal language, the statement declared that Giovanni Perri:

> is the legal next of kin and requests that the remains of Pvt. Luigi Perri be returned to Perri, Giovanni, whose address is Castrolibero, Cosenza, at the expense of the United States Government for delivery to him . . .

It is not known why Giovanni submitted this statement that completely contradicted his statement of consent dated the previous November. It may even imply that brother Michael had grown tired of waiting for a response from Giovanni and so created one for him. Nevertheless, on 23 March, Capt. Charles A. Morrow, Quartermaster Corps, wrote to Giovanni:

> We are pleased to inform you that your wishes have been made of record and will be complied with, provided the Italian Government authorizes the entry of the body in Italy. All exhumation costs and other expenses, including transportation to your home, will be paid by the American Government; burial expenses are to be borne by you.

On 23 March, the American Graves Registration Service in Europe wrote to the Quartermaster General in Washington, DC, stating:

> Reference letter from your office dated November 5th, 1920 . . . to these Headquarters, wherein it was directed that we communicate with the next of kin of [Luigi Perri], you are advised that reply has been received from Mr. Giovanni Perri . . . together with a sworn affidavit as to the prior residence of the deceased prior to enlisting in the U.S. Army . . . indicating that it is the desire of the father that the body be shipped to his address in Italy for final burial.

Of note here is that this letter includes erroneous reference to Luigi Perri's "father," who was, in fact, deceased. Probably the American Graves Registration Service in Europe was unaware of almost simultaneous ongoing correspondence that contradicted its decision. On 12 April, Perri's body was shipped to Paris; it arrived there two days later.

On 19 April, Michael Perri, frustrated at not having heard anything since early February, wrote again to Maj. Pierce. Referencing and enclosing copies of previous correspondence, Michael incredulously states:

With these papers I am also enclosing copy of a letter I have just received bearing the date of March 23, 1921, which indicates that there is some movement under way to ship the remains to Italy. I have previously furnished you with letter from my oldest brother, Giovanni Perri, consenting to the return of the body to me at Chicago, and I do not understand the conflicting instructions contained in the letter of March 23rd. Will you not kindly straighten the matter out so that the remains of Luigi Perri will be shipped to me . . . as per your letter of February 4th, and I would be glad to hear from you in this connection as early as possible.

A month later, Michael's frustration bubbled forth again in a letter to Pierce:

For ready reference I am enclosing a copy of my letter of April 19th to you written just one month ago today to which reply has not yet been received. May I not have an answer within the next few days?

Red tape is evident in the quartermaster general's office letter to Michael dated 26 May:

[Y]ou are advised that the policy under which this office must operate requires that it must comply with the request of the legal next of kin as regards the disposition of a body.

Under the date of November 5, 1920, this office communicated with the representative of the Graves Registration Service, Europe, and advice has been received that under date of March 13th your older brother, Mr. Giovanni Perri, requested the body be shipped to him in Italy.

This office regrets that it cannot comply with the letter of February 4, 1921, forwarded to you by the Hoboken office to the effect that the remains of your brother would be shipped to you for private burial, and trusts that it will meet with your approval to have the body shipped to his native land.

The next letters were queries and answers between Michael and the quartermaster general's office that crossed each other in the mail dated late May and early June 1921. At this point there is a perplexing, unexplained one-year gap in correspondence.

The next letter is dated 29 July 1922, when Michael wrote again to the quartermaster general's office. He included copies of pertinent letters and file numbers, then tried once again for a favorable resolution:

I have since been in communication with Giovanni Perri who is located at Castrolibero, Italy, and he has since consented to the removal and shipping of the body of Luigi Perri to me at Chicago, Illinois, and I am informed that the body has not yet been removed to Italy as contemplated in communication dated March 13th. . . . What I would like to have you now advise me is in just what form I shall secure and furnish you consent from Giovanni Perri to removal of the body to the United States and the abrogation of the communication of March 13th, 1921. Your very early attention to this matter will be much appreciated.

The quartermaster general's office replied to Michael on 8 August 1922:

In reply to your letter of July 29th, I regret that it is now too late to accept your request for the return of the remains . . . to this country [US] for final interment. August 15, 1921, was designated the date beyond which no changes of requests for the return of bodies would be accepted . . .

Should Mr. Giovanni Perri . . . desire to have the remains of Private Perri left in France for permanent burial in one of the American Cemeteries to be maintained in that country, he should so advise the Chief, American Graves Registration Service, Q.M.C. in Europe . . . with the least possible delay.

The file is, for all practical purposes, closed by the simple, bilingual affidavit of receipt dated 19 October 1922:

Received this date from Thomas E. McDonald, Convoyer, the remains of the following soldier and an American flag: Perri, Luigi, 1391161, Pvt. Co. G, 132nd Inf. Signed on above date at Castrolibero, Cosenza [signature of Giovanni Perri].

Thus ends a story that must have been repeated many times with soldiers from many different countries. It is obvious that the best intentions of the War Department could not always overcome the confusion generated by language barriers, slow mail, and changing human desires.

For the Doughboys returning home safely, and even for those who never left the United States, their stories had happier endings. Yet sometimes they, too, would meet with frustration and disappointment as they tried to return to civilian life.

John T. McEnteggart, a twenty-three-year-old native of Ireland, enlisted barely one month after the declaration of war. McEnteggart, along with others in Clayton, New Mexico, signed up in Company G, 1st New Mexico Infantry, New Mexico National Guard. Together they were sent to Logan, New Mexico, to guard a railroad bridge on the Rock Island line. By August he was in California, where his unit became

Detail from the Pennsylvania Veteran's Compensation Application filled out on behalf of Pvt. Michelangelo Apolito by his father, Leonardo Apolito, in Italy. Pvt. Apolito was killed in action on 29 October 1918, while serving in the 79th Division. This portion shows that Leonardo Apolito's information was checked and certified by Felix Martini, Department Adjutant for the American Legion, Department of Italy. Felix Martini was living in New York when he entered the Army during the war. *Courtesy Michelangelo Apolito, Pennsylvania Veteran's Compensation Application, and Felix Martini, Statement of Service Card, New York*

The Pennsylvania Veteran's Compensation Application filed by Robert Banks, formerly of the 407th Service Battalion, an African American unit in the Services of Supply. Banks, originally from the island of St. Thomas in the West Indies, was serving time in Dauphin County Jail at the time of application and was awarded $170 for his seventeen months spent in uniform. *Courtesy Pennsylvania Archives*

The military service extract for Patrick Healy, the Irish-born soldier whose draft registration card was shown earlier. By this point the Army had settled on "Healy" as the correct spelling of his surname. He was severely wounded by machine gun fire during the fighting in the Bois des Ogons in early October 1918 as a member of the 80th Division. *Courtesy the Rhodes and Smergalski families*

part of the 115th Headquarters and Military Police, 40th Division.[5]

On 1 January 1918, while performing guard duty in San Diego, McEnteggart became ill. Diagnosed with pulmonary tuberculosis of both lungs, he was discharged and given government compensation since he was disabled in the line of duty. McEnteggart fortunately soon found work at a bank, but this did not last long: "I got work in the First National Bank in Clayton and after being there a while was turned loose because the president found out I was a T. B. [case] . . ." From August 1918 to June 1919, McEnteggart entered a series of hospitals until finally being discharged as an "arrested case."

Writing to the New Mexico State Historical Service in reply to their request for service information in November 1919, McEnteggart's concern for his situation is evident:

> Can you tell me if the State of New Mexico has done anything in regards to the soldiers[?] The reason I ask this is I see where several states are giving bonuses etc. or can you tell me if there is any means of finding out as to where I can file on a piece of land[?]

There were hard-luck stories everywhere. Angelo Biscardi was born in Italy in 1888.[6] Biscardi came to the United States and was living in Chicago in 1915, when he decided to return to Italy to bring his wife and child back with him to America. While he was in Italy that country declared war on Germany, so Biscardi was caught in the Italian draft. While in the Italian army serving in the Alps, Biscardi was seriously wounded and medically discharged. In March 1917, he returned to America in time to register for the draft in June. At that time Biscardi listed his prior service with the Italian army and claimed exemption because he was the sole support of his wife, child, and mother; in addition, he was an alien. Despite this claim, Biscardi was drafted and reported for duty in April 1918. Sent overseas as a replacement, he was assigned to the 4th Infantry Regiment, 3rd Division. On 6 October 1918, Biscardi was severely wounded during the Meuse-Argonne Offensive. The notation on his statement of service card only hints at the horror and suffering he must have experienced: "Bayonet W. [wound] rt. Side Sh [shell] W. rt. Eye." After spending time in military hospitals, Biscardi returned to the United States in February 1919. One source indicates that his wife and child had died of influenza during his time in service, while another indicates he was divorced. In any event, personal and physical tragedy continued to plague him; unable to work at his previous job as a laborer due to his weakened physical condition, he moved to Chicago to find work. A May 1919 newspaper article states:

> Angelo Biscardi, bearing seven wounds received in the war, the *Croix de Guerre*, and honorable discharge papers from the Italian and United States armies, is walking the streets of Chicago seeking employment.

At some point he found work as a barber in Chicago. Sadly, a final tragedy struck soon thereafter. Biscardi died at his home in Chicago on 22 March 1920. The cause of death was listed as "Asphyxiation, Illuminating gas—accidental." It is well known that many returning servicemen, unable to cope with the horrors of what they had been through and unable to adjust to civilian society, committed suicide throughout the 1920s and 1930s. Perhaps Angelo Biscardi, wounded veteran of two armies, was one such person.

Also numbering among those needing help was Pasquale Bucciarelli, a twenty-three-year-old barber from Italy who enlisted on 17 June 1917. Initially assigned to the 37th Infantry Regiment, he was soon transferred to the 16th Infantry Regiment, 1st Division. As part of that vaunted Regular Army division, Bucciarelli saw plenty of combat. On his Pennsylvania Veterans Compensation application filled out in 1934, Bucciarelli listed his campaigns: Ansauville sector, Cantigny, Soissons, Saizerais sector, St. Mihiel, and Meuse-Argonne. He also listed his wounds: "G.S.W. [gun shot wound] right shoulder 2/26/18, Gassed 10/9/18, fractured nose the last part of October 1918." This is surely more than enough for any one man's service. Bucciarelli appended a poignant note to his application, one that could have been written by many AEF veterans at this time:

Now returned safely from France and wearing the patch of the 80th Division on his left shoulder, Turkish-born but ethnically Armenian Hagop Nerses Chopourian poses for a somber-looking portrait with a friend. While serving with the 315th Machine Gun Battalion, Chopourian was credited with participation in the Somme, St. Mihiel, and Meuse-Argonne Campaigns, as well as the defensive sectors of Limey, Artois (in Picardy), and Bethincourt (in Lorraine).

If it's possible to be included among the first [to receive a veteran's bonus], will be greatly appreciated because I am in need of it very badly.[7]

Not every story had a sad ending; taking a different direction was Bernard R. Kirchof, whose story sheds light on a little-known aspect of the US Army during and after the war.[8] Born in Germany in September 1899, Kirchof was employed as a "clerical worker, stenographer, and billing clerk" when the United States entered the war. Seventeen-year-old Kirchof immediately enlisted on 6 April 1917. Sent to Fort Barry, at the entrance to San Francisco Bay, as part of the 15th Company, Coast Artillery Corps, Kirchof soon became a "1st Class Gunner." He also served in Battery D, 40th Artillery Brigade, Railway, and along the way was promoted to corporal and sergeant.

The 40th was slated to go overseas, and according to Kirchof, "Was scheduled for overseas and arrived at Camp Upton, New York, with all our baggage on board transport when Armistice was signed." But this was not the end of Kirchof's military career. With almost four million men to be outprocessed and discharged, the Army was in dire need of qualified clerks to handle the necessary paperwork. Kirchof, with his clerical background, was a natural fit: "Was discharged as an enlisted man to accept appointment as Army Field Clerk March 21, 1919, but still in service . . . Will be in service continuously until completion of the demobilization." Army field clerks were specialists holding rank roughly equivalent to modern-day warrant officers. In this capacity Kirchof assisted with demobilization paperwork at Camp Grant and at the demobilization camp at the Presidio in San Francisco.

The old country had a certain pull on foreign-born soldiers, sometimes stronger in some men than in others. Italian-born men seemed to be particularly inclined to return to their native soil, at least for periodic visits. One man, Joseph J. Attura, paved the way for fellow Italian American veterans to return to Italy.[9] Attura, a native of Rome, served in Headquarters Company, 18th Infantry Regiment, 1st Division. He was severely wounded in May 1918 but rejoined his regiment and participated in the rest of the 18th's battles.

Attura was discharged in 1919; in 1920, he moved back to Italy, where he married, started a family, and opened a tobacco shop. In 1925, Attura and F. B. Gigliotti, another AEF veteran living in Italy, started Rome Post Number 1, American Legion, Department of Italy. In addition to furthering the camaraderie the men had established during their military service in the United States, the new post provided a very practical service. Many veterans in Italy were denied reentry to the United States because the State Department had deemed them to be officially repatriated and ineligible for immediate resumption of their US residence, or even citizenship. The men and their families had a hard time accessing benefits, such as state veterans' bonuses and insurance and pension payments. Therefore, "The American Legion's Department of Italy was established principally to address these wrongs."

How the American Legion Post in Italy facilitated the application for and receipt of benefits is illustrated in the case of Pennsylvania's veterans' compensation. When this measure was approved, qualified veterans, or surviving family members, had to

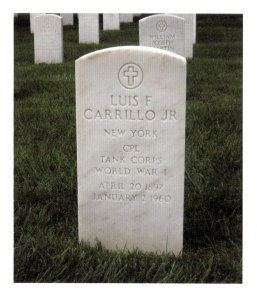

The final resting place in Fort Harrison National Cemetery of Luis F. Carrillo Jr., born in Bogatá, Colombia. Carrillo served in Company B of the 329th Tank Battalion and was a sergeant by war's end.

Resting far from his native Denmark but not forgotten, Sgt. Axel P. Christoffersen is buried among Civil War, WWI, and WWII soldiers in a very small cemetery in Seven Pines, Virginia. At the time of this photograph, Christoffersen's grave had just been visited by family members from Denmark and decorated with a small Danish flag and a pamphlet with pictures of his family and hometown.

fill out the Veteran's Compensation Application attesting to their identity and service. This, in turn, had to be notarized, and a certificate of identification had to be completed. Many Pennsylvania World War I veterans or their surviving family members lived in Italy. Post Number 1, American Legion, Department of Italy, served to certify each veteran's case, as appropriate, and facilitate submission of the application. The ability to obtain proof of service during the period was critical; many states had decided on their own to award bonuses to eligible veterans.

Another example of the importance of the American Legion post in Italy is the case of Italian-born Benedetto Sicilia.[10] Sicilia came to the United States in 1913 and joined other members of his extended family in Chicago and Kenosha, Wisconsin. In August 1918, Sicilia was drafted and reported for duty in the 5th Training Battalion, 158th Depot Brigade at Camp Sherman. On 6 December 1918, Sicilia was discharged, and he returned to Kenosha to continue his life. Sometime in 1919 Sicilia was awarded a Wisconsin veteran's bonus, the amount of which was determined by each man's length of service and on overseas service. Sicilia's bonus came to fifty dollars, probably the minimum amount awarded. Sometime in 1921 Sicilia returned to Italy, where he married and started a family.

On 29 January 1926, Sicilia died in Italy, and his widow filed a pension claim based upon her deceased husband's wartime US military service and his War Risk Insurance policy. In 1947, 1949, and again in 1951, Sicilia's widow filled out bilingual Veterans Administration claims forms certifying that she still qualified for pension payments, which amounted to about forty-two dollars annually. She had received assistance from the American Legion, Department of Italy, in filling out at least the 1947 forms. This was surely not an isolated case.

Interestingly, many of the men who had become US citizens either during their time in the military or immediately thereafter and then returned to Italy to take up residence had their citizenship revoked by the US State Department.

An example is Filiberto Morelli, who was wounded on the war's last day while serving in the 130th Infantry Regiment, 33rd Division. Morelli had his citizenship revoked because, "Petitioner established a permanent residence in Italy within 5 years after being admitted to citizenship."[11]

The impact of their service remained with the men after their discharge from the military. William Adair, a thirty-two-year-old immigrant from Scotland serving in the 27th Engineer Regiment, filled out a New Mexico State Historical Service questionnaire shortly after his discharge. After giving a brief resumé of his travels in the Army, ending with his arrival at the front during the Meuse-Argonne Offensive, Adair concluded: "Please excuse me but I can't tell you anymore of my experiences in the meantime may do it at a future date Hope you don't take this as an insult for them times are to fresh in my memory yet."[12]

What can be said in summation about the hundreds of thousands of foreign-born soldiers serving in the US military during the war? Many of them were exceptionally brave, a few of them were cowards, and the vast majority of them served honorably, with no particular distinction. They entered the service both willingly and by force of prosecution. Some were "just off the boat," without the ability to speak or understand a word of English. Others were educated men and women who excelled in academics. They served in every theater of war and in every type of military unit. They won every available award for bravery and service, and they faced every hardship more or less as cheerfully as their native-born comrades. Many of them became US citizens during their period of service. Most of them returned home to their family and friends and became productive citizens. Others, for whatever reason, returned to their place of birth to live out their lives.

During the First World War, there was a very popular song with lyrics that described "a long, long trail a-winding into the land of my dreams."[13] In these chapters we have tried to give a sense of the foreign-born men and women who walked that long, long trail, and one hopes that most did find the land of their dreams. Along that journey, by sharing their stories and showing their faces, we have attempted to bring them to life for you. But what speaks most eloquently of their service are the countless Christian crosses and Stars of David that mark the graves of those who gave the last full measure of devotion to their adopted country. Above the entrances to many of the cemeteries where they now rest can usually be found Gen. Pershing's epitaph for them: "Time will not dim the glory of their deeds."

# ENDNOTES

**Foreword**

1. Committee on Public Information, *American Loyalty*, p. 3.
2. Tiebout, *305th Infantry*, pp. 19–20.
3. 77th Division Association, *The Seventy-Seventh Division*, p. 8.
4. Alvin York Diary, Alvin York Institute, http://www2.york.k12.tn.us.
5. Johns, *Camp Travis*, p. 63.
6. Hoffman, *The Famous 42nd "Rainbow,"* p. 8.
7. Mead, *The Doughboys*, p. 368, and *Gas Attack*, p. 20.
8. March, *Nation at War*, pp. 23–26.

**Chapter 1.**

1. Price, *Washington's Nine Months at War*, p. 48.
2. Bacarella, *Lincoln's Foreign Legion*, p. 231.
3. McPherson, *What They Fought For*, via Portland State University, http://www.upa.pdx.edu/.
4. Lonn, *Foreigners*, pp. 575–582.
5. Wiley and Milhollen, *They Who Fought Here*, p. 8.
6. Dinnerstein, Nichols, Reimers, *Natives and Strangers*, p. 123.
7. Iorizzo and Mondello, *The Italian Americans*, p. 218.
8. Nugent, *Crossings,* pp. 84–94. This work provides a summary of this immigration and the difficulties in determining precise numbers of the various ethnic and national groups involved.
9. Ibid., pp. 101–105.
10. Ibid., p. 65. This figure represents author Belmonte's attempt to reconcile different figures as given by Germany and the United States.
11. Ibid., p. 46.
12. Ibid., p. 48.
13. Ibid., pp. 56–57.
14. Dinnerstein, *Natives and Strangers*, p. 210.
15. Ibid., p. 211.
16. Ibid., p. 212.
17. *Spanish American War Veteran's Compensation File*. Dept. of Military and Veteran's Affairs, Record Group 19. Pennsylvania State Archives, Ancestry.com. *Pennsylvania, Spanish War Compensation, 1898–1934*. This database covers men who entered service from Pennsylvania and later applied for that state's compensation for military veterans. Author Belmonte conducted an online search for men born in the various nations listed. It is important to note that this method is imperfect but probably gives an overall accurate picture of the situation with men who applied for veterans' compensation. Furthermore, the database covers men who actually applied for compensation and not all veterans.
18. For Joseph Barchi: Service Records, National Archives at St. Louis, National Personnel Records Center, St. Louis, MO; For Barchi's passport application: National Archives and Records Administration (NARA); Washington, DC; NARA Series: *Passport Applications,*

*January 2, 1906–March 31, 1925*, at Ancestry.com; for Jan Soer, see various databases on Ancestry.com.

19. Nugent, *Crossings*, p. 151.


**Chapter 2.**

1. Center of Military History, *United States Order of Battle* , vol. 3, pt. 1, p. 368.

2. Woodward, *The American*, p. 46.

3. Beaver, *Newton D. Baker*, pp. 30–31.

4. Center of Military History, *Order of Battle, vol. 3, pt. 1*, pp. 369–370.

5. Ibid., p. 370.

6. US Provost Marshal General, *Final Report*, p. 9.

7. Center of Military History, *Order of Battle* , vol. 3, pt. 1, p. 372.

8. *New York Times*, 21 June 1921.

9. US Provost Marshal General, *Final Report*, pp. 9–13.

10. Mead, *The Doughboys: America and the First World War,* p. 366; Center of Military History, *Order of Battle, vol. 3, pt. 1*, pp. 367–409.

11. *The New York Times*, 26 May 1917.

12. US Provost Marshal General, *Second Report*, p. 95.

13. Ibid., p. 96.

14. Ibid., p. 97.

15. *Pennsylvania, WWI Veterans Service*, Ancestry.com, 2015.

16. US Provost Marshal General, *Second Report*, p. 99.

17. Ibid., p. 100.

18. See, for example, Military Service Records, Filiberto Settino, Report of Physical Examination, National Archives and Records Administration, St. Louis, MO.

19. US Provost Marshal General, *Second Report*, p. 14. Historian Robert H. Ferrell stated that 4,271,150 men and women served in the Army by war's end. See also Ferrell, *Woodrow Wilson*, p. 18.


**Chapter 3.**

1. Cushing and Stone, *Vermont*, p. 4.

2. Pixley, *Wisconsin*, p. 42.

3. Robinson, *Forging the Sword,* pp. 11–12.

4. Cushing and Stone, *Vermont,* p. 5.

5. Fortescue, "Training the New Armies," p. 425.

6. Ibid.

7. Cole and Howells, *Thirty-Seventh Division*, pp. 187–188.

8. Cooper and Smith, *Citizens as Soldiers*, p. 202.

9. Ibid., p. 203.

10. Ibid., pp. 203–207.

11. Thisted, *Pershing's Pioneer*, p. 19.

12. Reilly, *Americans All*, pp. 20–25.

13. Divisional Officers, *History of 82nd Division*, pp. 1–2.

14. Alvin York Diary, February 1918, Courtesy of the Alvin York Institute, http://www2.york. k12.tn.us.
15. York Diary, March 1918.
16. Ibid.
17. York Diary, July 1918.
18. Divisional Officers, *History of 82nd Division*, p. 2.
19. Johns, *Camp Travis*, pp. 225–230, 312.
20. Kennedy, *Over Here*, pp. 187–188, and Ferrell, *Woodrow Wilson*, p. 20.
21. Powell, *The Army*, p. 373.
22. *Extracts from General Orders and Bulletins, War Department,* pp. 5–6. Accessed via books. google.com.
23. Center of Military History, *Order of Battle, vol. 3, pt. 3*, pp. 1277–1308. Accessed via http://www.Hathitrust.org.
24. *Extracts from General Orders and Bulletins, War Department*, May 1918, p. 6.
25. Ibid., p. 7.
26. War Department, *Operation of Development Battalions*, p. 6.
27. Ibid., p. 8.
28. Ibid., pp. 8–9.
29. Magoffin, "Morale Work," January–December 1920.
30. Judy, *A Soldier's Diary*, pp. 56, 72.
31. See Aceto's and Tenuta's Statement of Service Cards, Wisconsin Veterans Museum, Madison, WI.
32. *Utah, Military Records, 1861–1970* (database online). Provo, UT: Ancestry.com, *Utah State Historical Society World War I Service Questionnaires*, via Ancestry.com.
33. New York State WWI Service Abstracts, via Ancestry.com.
34. *Evening Star*, 2 October 1917.
35. *Pennsylvania, Spanish War Compensation, 1898–1934*, via Ancestry.com.
36. New York State WWI Service Abstracts via Ancestry.com, and Crane, *The Medical Department*, pp. 630–631.
37. Reba G. Cameron citation courtesy of First Division Museum at Cantigny, Wheaton, IL.
38. Committee on Classification of Personnel, *The Personnel System of the United States Army, vol. I*, p. 520.
39. All data regarding development battalion soldiers from Kenosha and Racine per Wisconsin Veterans Museum, Statement of Service cards, and databases on Ancestry.com.

**Chapter 4**
1. Cole and Howells, *Thirty-Seventh Division*, pp. 392–393.
2. Ibid., p. 393.
3. US Provost Marshal General, *Second Report*, pp. 104–105.
4. Ibid.
5. Ibid., p. 105.
6. Cole and Howells, *Thirty-Seventh Division*, p. 391.
7. Ibid.
8. Ibid., p. 393.

9. Ibid.

10. Ibid., p. 391.

11. Ohio, *Official Roster of Ohio*, p. 8351.

12. Ibid., pp. 8789–8791.

13. Cutchins, *Twenty-Ninth Division*, pp. 43–44.

14. Courtesy Camp Zachary Taylor Historical Society of Louisville, KY.

15. Belmonte, *Calabrian Americans in the US Military During World War I: Cosenza-Area Immigrants*, vol. 1 (CreateSpace, 2017).

16. States Publication Society, *Eighty-Sixth Division*, p. 76.

17. *New York Times*, 23 May 1918.

18. Huidekoper, *33rd Division, vol. 1*, pp. 16–32.

19. Barber, *Seventy-Ninth Division*, p. 37.

20. Center of Military History, *Order of Battle, vol. 3, pt. 2*, p. 748.

21. Ibid., pp. 753–754.

22. Ibid., p. 791.

23. *Special Regulations No. 103, Students' Army Training Corps*, p. 5.

24. *Pennsylvania, WWI Veterans Service and Compensation Files*, via Ancestry.com.

25. Meyer. *New Mexico, World War I Records, 1917–1919* [database online]. Provo, UT: Ancestry.com, 2014. Original data: New Mexico Council of Defense.

26. Enriquez. *New Mexico, World War I Records*, via Ancestry.com.

27. Haight, *Racine County*, p. 582 (available online via http://www.hathitrust.org).

**Chapter 5.**

1. Beaver, *Newton D. Baker,* pp. 85–86.

2. Stewart, *American Military History. vol. II*, pp. 8–11.

3. Information courtesy Bert J. Cunningham, historian, 69th Infantry Regiment, Regimental Headquarters, New York City.

4. Johnson, *Roster of the Rainbow*, pp. 174–202.

5. Ibid., pp. 35–120.

6. Beaver, *Newton D. Baker*, p. 85.

7. Nenninger, "Tactical Dysfunction, p. 180.

8. Ibid.

9. American Legion, *Source Records*, p. 33.

10. *World War Records, First Division*, Operations Reports, vol. XIV, courtesy 1st Division Museum at Cantigny, Wheaton, IL.

11. Stallings, *The Doughboys*, pp. 70–71.

12. Telegram to Foreign Army Section, 19 May 1918, in *World War Records, First Division*, German Documents, Sommerviller, Ansauville, and Cantigny Sectors, vol. I; Letter from Lt. Col. Barnwell Legge, 13 July 1919, courtesy First Division Museum at Cantigny, Wheaton, Illinois.

13. Wilson, *Maneuver and Firepower*, pp. 10–20.

14. Barber, *Seventy-Ninth Division*, pp. 25–26.

15. *The Stars & Stripes*, 28 February 1918.

16. Keith diary, 37th Division, in private collection.

17. *New Mexico, World War I Records*, via Ancestry.com.

18. Martin, *Twenty-Eighth Division*, p. 292.

19. Ibid., pp. 375–376.

20. March, *Nation at War*, pp. 5–6.

21. Nenninger, "Tactical Dysfunction," p. 180.

22. All information on Carmine Chiappetta from Veterans Administration claims paperwork and draft registration form. See also, Belmonte, *Calabrian-Americans in the US Military During World War I.*

23. Carmine Chiappetta from Veterans Administration claims paperwork.

24. Ibid.

25. Ibid.

26. All information on Vincent Presta, courtesy of Rose Presta Pennington, 16 January 2005.

27. Ibid.

28. For Carmine Belmonte's birth information, see Marano Marchesato, Calabria, Italy; birth, death, and marriage information comes from Family History Library microfilms. For his military service see Carmine Belmonte, Statement of Service card, Illinois Adjutant General's Office, Springfield, IL. Also Military Personnel Records Center, National Archives, St. Louis, MO. For the 1st Construction Company, see "1st Construction Company, A. S." Typescript history dated 23 January 1919; Information Section, Air Service, AEF. See also Belmonte, *Calabrian-Americans in the US Military During World War I.*

29. George Campbell information courtesy 1st Division Museum at Cantigny, Wheaton, IL.

30. Belmonte, *Days of Perfect Hell*, p. 96.

31. Lebow, *A Grandstand Seat*, p. 110.

32. Cutchins, *An Amateur*, pp. 112–113.

33. Beatrice MacDonald information courtesy First Division Museum at Cantigny, Wheaton, IL.

**Chapter 6.**

1. Seal, *116th U.S. Infantry Regiment,* p.88.

2. Jake Allex information and Medal of Honor citation courtesy of the Congressional Medal of Honor Society.

3. Johannes Anderson information and Medal of Honor citation courtesy of the Congressional Medal of Honor Society.

4. Rubin, *The Last of the Doughboys*, pp. 241–243.

5. Raymond Buma information courtesy Rogier van de Hoef.

6. Louis Cukela information and Medal of Honor citations courtesy of the Congressional Medal of Honor Society and the USMC History Division.

7. *Stars and Stripes*, 14 February 1919.

8. Stallings, *The Doughboys*, pp. 156–157.

9. George Dilboy information and Medal of Honor citation courtesy of the Congressional Medal of Honor Society.

10. Reilly, *Americans All,* and Stephen L. Harris, *Duffy's War.*

11. Matej Kocak information and Medal of Honor citation courtesy of the Congressional Medal of Honor Society.
12. Information courtesy USMC History Division.
13. General Walter Krueger information courtesy US Army Center for Military History homepage, http://WWW.History.Army.mil.
14. Berger Loman information courtesy Arlington National Cemetery, https://Arlingtoncemetery. mil, and Medal of Honor citation courtesy of the Congressional Medal of Honor Society.
15. James I. Mestrovitch information and Medal of Honor citation courtesy of the Congressional Medal of Honor Society.
16. 77th Division Association, *Seventy-Seventh Division*, p. 183, and *New York, Abstracts of World War I Military Service, 1917–1919* via Ancestry.com.
17. Cutchins, *Twenty-Ninth Division*, p. 476, and US World War I Draft Registration Cards, 1917–1918 via Ancestry.com.
18. Joseph Thompson information and Medal of Honor citation courtesy of the Congressional Medal of Honor Society.
19. Michael Valente information and Medal of Honor citation courtesy of the Congressional Medal of Honor Society.
20. Louis van Iersel information and Medal of Honor citation courtesy of the Congressional Medal of Honor Society
21. Reidar Waaler information and Medal of Honor citation courtesy of the Congressional Medal of Honor Society.

**Chapter 7.**
1. Liberty Loan Program Pamphlet, *What the War Will Do*, p. 10.
2. Flint Daily Journal, *Honor Roll*, p. 76.
3. Ibid., pp. 76–78.
4. Ibid., p. 78.
5. Information supplied by the First Division Museum at Cantigny, Wheaton, IL.
6. Gentile, *Americans All!*, p. 106.
7. Ibid.
8. Cornebise, *War as Advertised*, p. 26.
9. Faribault County, *In the World War*, p. 179–180.
10. Information on the Virginia State Guard units is courtesy the Virginia National Guard archives.

**Chapter 8**
1. MacNider, *Conscientious*, p. 4.
2. Thomas van der Veen Distinguished Service Medal Citation from US Army General Orders 87, W. D., 1919.
3. Much of the credit for tracking these Dutch Doughboys must go to Rogier van de Hoef, who is dedicated to keeping their memory, and all of the 4th Division's memory, alive. The authors are indebted to him for his determination in researching all the Doughboys of the 4th Division and the Dutch Doughboys of the 4th Division in particular.

4. Study of DeLuca surname information from New York State Archives, Pennsylvania State Archives, Utah State Archives, via Ancestry.com, and *Ohio Soldiers in WWI, 1917–1918*, Provo, UT: Ancestry.com, 2005.

5. All the information on the Pellegrini brothers is found in Belmonte, "The Pellegrini Brothers of Chicago: Italian American Tailors Become Soldiers during World War I," paper presented at the 16th Annual Conference on Illinois History, 25–26 September 2014, Springfield, IL. See also, Belmonte, *Calabrian-Americans in the US Military During World War I*.

6. Research on Japanese draftees, courtesy New York State Archives.

7. *The New York Times*, 4 May 1919.

8. Manuel Gonzales, *New Mexico, World War I Records*, via Ancestry.com.

9. Manuel Gonzales letter to mother, dated 19 July 1918, *New Mexico, World War I Records*, via Ancestry.com.

10. Frank Gouin, *New Mexico, World War I Records*, via Ancestry.com.

11. Ibid.

12. Martone unpublished manuscript, courtesy Virginia War Museum, Newport News, VA.

13. Fosdick and Allen, *Keeping Our Fighters*, p. 158.

14. Ibid.

15. US Department of the Army, *American Military Government of Occupied Germany*, p. 215.

16. Ibid., p. 209.

17. For more on foreign-born soldiers and the Army's efforts to train them stateside, see Ford, *Americans All! Foreign-Born Soldiers in World War I*.

18. National Archives, *WWI Draft Registration Records, 1917–1918,* via Ancestry.com.

19. Ibid.

20. All information for the Syrian-born doughboys is from the *Pennsylvania, WWI Veterans Service and Compensation Files*, via Ancestry.com.

21. *Utah, Military Records, 1861–1970* via Ancestry.com.

22. *Pennsylvania, WWI Veterans Service and Compensation Files*, via Ancestry.com.

23. All information for the Albanian-born Doughboys is from the New York and Pennsylvania State Archives and the *Order of Battle of the United States Land Forces in the World War, American Expeditionary Forces: Divisions, vol. 2*.

24. US Selective Service System. *World War I Selective Service System Draft Registration Cards, 1917–1918*. Washington, DC: National Archives and Records Administration. M1509, 4,582 rolls. For Ferraro's arrival in the United States, see Passenger and Crew Lists of Vessels Arriving at New York, New York, 1897–1957; Records of the Immigration and Naturalization Service; National Archives, Washington, DC.

25. For Ferraro's declaration of intention, see University of Wisconsin-Parkside Archives and Area Research Center: Eugenio Ferraro, Declaration of Intention. For his military service record, see National Archives and Records Administration, National Personnel Records Center, St. Louis, MO. Navy Personnel Records, Eugenio Ferraro file.

26. National Archives and Records Administration (NARA); Washington, DC; *Soundex Index to Naturalization Petitions for the United States District and Circuit Courts, Northern District of Illinois and Immigration and Naturalization Service District 9, 1840–1950 (M1285)*.

27. Rudolph Ferraro, Kenosha, WI, telephone interview with author Belmonte, 16 January 2013.

28. Year: *1920*; Census Place: *Great Lakes, Lake, Illinois*; Roll: *T625_381*; Page: *19A*; Enumeration District: *263*; Image: *909*.

29. Marano Marchesato, Civil Records, LDS Microfilm Number 1608135, *Nati*, via http://www.rootsweb.ancestry.com.

30. For Spizzirri's military service records, see National Archives and Records Administration, National Personnel Records Center, St. Louis, MO: Navy Personnel Records, Anthony Spizzirri file.

31. Marano Marchesato, Civil Records, op. cit. For Bruno's immigration, see Passenger and Crew Lists of Vessels Arriving at New York, New York, 1897–1957; Records of the Immigration and Naturalization Service; National Archives, Washington, DC. Year: *1902*; Arrival; Microfilm Serial: *T715*; Microfilm Roll: *285*; Line: *6*; Page Number: *32*.

32. For Bruno's military service record, see National Archives and Records Administration, National Personnel Records Center, Navy Personnel Records, Louis Bruno file.

33. Faribault County, *In the World War*, p. 23.

34. City of Rochester, *World War Service Record*, p. 416.

35. *The New York Times*, 22 September 1918.

36. Ibid., 9 August 1918.

37. US Government, *The Official U.S. Bulletin,* Issues 402–451. Published 5 October 1918.

38. Ibid.

39. Shay, *Sky Pilots*, pp. 171–178.

40. http://www.worldwar1.com/dbc/hello.htm

41. Wiegers, "The 'Hello Girls' of the Great War" pp. 4–5.

42. *The Twenty-Niner* newsletter, Summer 1990 edition.

## Chapter 9

1. Stallings, *The Doughboys*, p. 6.

2. Cutchins, *Twenty-Ninth Division*, p. 119.

3. Ernest Northey: *New Mexico, World War I Records, 1917–1919*, via Ancestry.com.

4. Ibid.

5. Bach and Hall, *The Fourth Division*, p. 233, and Robert Koehn, Collection of letters, 1918–1919, letter to family dated 25 November 1918.

6. *New Mexico, World War I Records, 1917–1919*, via Ancestry.com.

7. Ernest Northey. *New Mexico, World War I Records, 1917–1919*, via Ancestry.com.

8. Ibid.

9. Cutchins, *Twenty-Ninth Division*, p. 247.

10. Ibid., p. 248.

11. Ibid., p. 249.

12. Reynolds and McLaughlin, *115th Infantry*, pp. 171–173.

13. George and Cooper, *Twenty-Sixth Division*, p. 19.

14. State Publication Society, *Eighty-Sixth Division*, p. 66.

15. Cutchins, *Twenty-Ninth Division*, pp. 263–263, and Burton, *600 Days' Service*, p. 194, and Barber, *Seventy-Ninth Division*, pp. 358–360, and Commanding General 88th, *88th Division*, pp. 97–102.

16. Burton, *600 Days' Service*, p. 80.

17. Reynolds and McLaughlin, *115th Infantry*, p. 195, and March, *The Nation at War*, p. 323.

18. Salvatore Rockette/Rucchetto's military service records courtesy National Archives, St. Louis, MO. See also, Belmonte, *Calabrian-Americans in the US Military During World War I*.

**Chapter 10**

1. Ernest Northey, *New Mexico, World War I Records, 1917–1919*, via Ancestry.com.

2. Eugenio Scarloto, Burial information file, National Archives and Records Administration, and Veterans Administration files, draft registration card via Ancestry.com, and statement of service card (courtesy Wisconsin Veterans Museum). See also, Belmonte, *Calabrian-Americans in the US Military During World War I*.

3. Luigi Perri, Burial information file, National Archives and Records Administration.

4. Davis, *The 132d Infantry*, unpaginated.

5. John McEnteggart, *New Mexico, World War I Records, 1917–1919*, via Ancestry.com.

6. Angelo Biscardi: Passenger list information compiled and retained by author Belmonte; statement of service card, Wisconsin Veterans Museum, Madison, WI; draft registration card via Ancestry.com; newspaper article, "Man Who Fought Under Two Flags Seeks Job Here," *Chicago Daily Tribune*, 25 May 1919, Section Two, page 21, scanned copy courtesy Vicky Zagame; State of Illinois, Certificate of Death number 12097. See also, Belmonte, *Calabrian-Americans in the US Military During World War I*.

7. Pasquale Bucciarelli, *Pennsylvania, WWI Veterans Service and Compensation Files*, via Ancestry.com.

8. Bernard Kirchof, *Utah Military Records, 1861–1970*, via Ancestry.com.

9. Joseph Attura, World War I Veterans Survey, US Army Heritage and Education Center, Carlisle Barracks, PA.

10. Benedetto Sicilia, US Department of Veterans Affairs, Pension File Number XC-655672.

11. Filiberto Morelli, *US Naturalization Record Indexes, 1791–1992*, via Ancestry.com. Also, his Statement of Service Card, Illinois Adjutant General's Office.

12. William Adair, *New Mexico, World War I Records, 1917–1919*, via Ancestry.com.

13. Words and lyrics to *There's a Long, Long Trail A-winding* by Stoddard King and Alonzo Elliott, published 1913-1914.

# BIBLIOGRAPHY

**Official Documents and Reports:**

American Expeditionary Forces, General Staff, General Headquarters. *Candid Comment on the American Soldier of 1917–1918 and Kindred Topics by the Germans*. Chaumont, France, 1919.

American Legion. *Source Records of the Great War*. Vol. VII. Edited by Charles H. Horne. Indianapolis, IN: American Legion, 1931.

Annual Report of the Adjutant General of the State of New York for the Year 1916. Albany, NY: J. B. Lyon, 1917.

Center of Military History. *United States Order of Battle of the United States Land Forces in the World War Zone of the Interior*. Vol. 3, Pt. 1, *Organization and Activities of the War Department*. Washington, DC: Center of Military History, US Army, 1988a.

Center of Military History. *United States Order of Battle of the United States Land Forces in the World War Zone of the Interior*. Vol. 3, Pt. 2, *Territorial Departments Tactical Divisions Organized in 1918 Posts, Camps, and Stations*. Washington, DC: Center of Military History, US Army, 1988b.

Committee on Classification of Personnel in the Army. *The Personnel System of the United States Army*. Vol. 1, *History of the Personnel System*. Washington, DC: US Government Printing Office, 1919.

Committee on Public Information. *American Loyalty by Citizens of German Descent*. Washington, DC: US Government Printing Office, 1917.

Crane, Maj. A. G., USA. T*he Medical Department of the United States Army in the World War*. Vol. XIII. Washington, DC: US Government Printing Office, 1927.

Cushing, John T., and Arthur F. Stone. *Vermont in the World War*. Burlington, VT: Free Press, 1928.

Davis, Arthur Kyle. *Virginia Military Organizations in the World War*. Publications, Source Volume V. Richmond, VA: Executive Committee of the Virginia War History Commission, 1927.

Fosdick, Raymond B., and Edward F. Allen. *Keeping Our Fighters Fit: For War and After*. Washington, DC: War Department Commission on Training Camp Activities, 1918.

Fraser, Brig. Gen. G. Angus. *Roster of the Men and Women Who Served in the Army or Naval Service of the United States or Its Allies from the State of North Dakota in the World War, 1917–1918*. Vols. 3 and 4, Bismarck, ND: Bismarck Tribune Company, 1931.

Greenfield, Kent Roberts, Robert R. Palmer, and Bell I. Wiley. *United States Army in World War II: The Army Ground Forces; The Organization of Combat Ground Troops*. Washington, DC: Center of Military History, US Army, 1987.

Hylton, Renee, and Robert K. Wright Jr. *A Brief History of the Militia and National Guard Departments of the Army and Air Force*. Washington, DC: Historical Services Division, Office of Public Affairs, National Guard Bureau, August 1993.

Liberty Loan Program Pamphlet. "What the War Will Do for America." New York: Samuel Untermeyer, 1918.

MacDonald, Charles B. *American Military History*. Army Historical Series 1. Washington, DC: Office of the Chief of Military History, US Army, 1989.

*Memoirs of the National Academy of Sciences*. Vol. XV. Washington, DC: Government Printing Office, 1921.

National Archives at St. Louis, National Personnel Records Center, St. Louis, MO. Military service records, various.

National Defense Act of 1916, Pub. L. 64–85, 39 Stat. 166, enacted 3 June 1916.

Ohio. *The Official Roster of Ohio, Soldiers, Sailors, and Marines in the World War 1917–18.* Vol. IX. Compiled under the direction of Governor of Ohio Vic Donehey. Columbus, OH: F. J. Heer, 1926.

Pershing, Gen. John J., USA Commander-in-Chief, American Expeditionary Forces. Report cabled to the Secretary of War, November 30, 1918. Corrected 10 January 1919.

Pixley, R. B. *Wisconsin in the World War.* Milwaukee, WI: Wisconsin War History Company, 1919.

Stewart, Richard W. *American Military History.* Vol. 1, *The United States Army and the Forging of a Nation, 1775–1917.* Army Historical Series. Washington, DC: Center of Military History, US Army, 2005.

Stewart, Richard W. *American Military History.* Vol. 2, *The United States Army in a Global Era, 1917–2008. Army Historical Series.* Washington, DC: Center of Military History, US Army, 2010.

US Department of the Army. *The War with Germany: A Statistical Summary.* 2d ed. Compiled by Colonel Leonard P. Ayres. Washington, DC: US Government Printing Office, 1919.

US Department of the Army. *American Military Government of Occupied Germany, 1918–1920: Report of the Officer in Charge of Civil Affairs, Third Army and American Forces Germany.* Washington, DC: US Government Printing Office, 1943.

US Department of the Army. *United States Army in the World War 1917–1919.* Vol. 9, *Military Operations of the American Expeditionary Forces.* Washington, DC: US Army Historical Division, 1948a.

US Department of the Army. *United States Army in the World War 1917–1919.* Vol. 12, *Reports of the Commander-in-Chief, A.E.F., Staff Sections and Services.* Washington, DC: US Army Historical Division, 1948b.

US Department of the Army. *The Army Lineage Book.* Vol. 2, *Infantry.* Washington, DC: US Government Printing Office, 1953.

US Department of the Army, Center of Military History. *American Armies and Battlefields in Europe.* Washington, DC: US Government Printing Office, 1995.

US Department of the Army, Quartermaster Corps School. *Operations of the Quartermaster Corps US Army during the World War, Monograph No. 9, Notes on Army, Corps and Division Quartermaster Activities in the American Expeditionary Forces–France.* Philadelphia: Quartermaster Corps School, Schuylkill Arsenal, undated.

US Government. *The Official U.S. Bulletin.* Issues 402–451. Published 5 October 1918.

US Provost Marshal General. *Second Report of the Provost Marshal General to the Secretary of War on the Operations of the Selective Service System to December 20, 1918.* Washington, DC: US Government Printing Office, 1919.

US Provost Marshal General. *Final Report of the Provost Marshal General to the Secretary of War on the Operations of the Selective Service System to July 13, 1919.* Washington, DC: US Government Printing Office, 1920.

War Department. *Order of Battle of the United States Land Forces in the World War.* Vol. 2, *American Expeditionary Forces: Divisions.* Washington, DC: US Government Printing Office, 1931–1949.

War Department. *Order of Battle of the United States Land Forces in the World War (1917–19)*. Vol. 3, *Zone of the Interior*. Washington, DC: US Government Printing Office, 1931–1949.

War Department, Office of the Adjutant General. *Extracts from General Orders and Bulletins, May 1918*. Washington, DC: US Government Printing Office: 1918.

War Department, Office of the Adjutant General. *Instructions concerning Operation of Development Battalions*. Washington, DC: US Government Printing Office: 1918.

Wisconsin Adjutant General's Office. *Regimental Muster and Descriptive Rolls, World War I*. Madison, WI: Wisconsin Veterans Museum, undated.


**Other Published Sources:**

Bacarella, Michael. *Lincoln's Foreign Legion: The 39th New York Infantry, the Garibaldi Guard*. Shippensburg, PA: White Mane, 1996.

Barnes, Alexander F. *In a Strange Land: The American Occupation of Germany, 1918–1923*. Atglen, PA: Schiffer Publishing Ltd., 2011.

Beamish, Richard J., and Francis A. March, Ph.D. *America's Part in the World War*. Philadelphia: John C. Winston, 1919.

Beaver, Daniel R. *Newton D. Baker and the American War Effort, 1917–1919*. Lincoln: University of Nebraska Press, 1966.

Belmonte, Peter L. *Days of Perfect Hell: The US 26th Infantry Regiment in the Meuse-Argonne Offensive, October–November 1918*. Atglen, PA: Schiffer Publishing Ltd., 2015.

Berry, Henry. *Make the Kaiser Dance*. Garden City, NY: Doubleday, 1978.

Bodnar, John. *The Transplanted: A History of Immigrants in Urban America*. Bloomington: Indiana University Press, 1987.

Butler, Capt. Alban, Jr. *"Happy Days!" A Humorous Narrative in Drawings of the Progress of American Arms, 1917–1919*. Washington, DC: Society of the First Division. A.E.F., 1928.

Cooper, Jerry, and Glenn Smith. *Citizens as Soldiers: A History of the North Dakota National Guard*. Fargo: North Dakota Institute for Regional Studies, North Dakota State University, 1986.

Cornebise, Alfred E. *War as Advertised: The Four Minute Men and America's Crusade, 1917–1918*. Philadelphia: American Philosophical Society, 1984.

Dalessandro, Robert J., and Michael G. Knapp. *Organization and Insignia of the American Expeditionary Force, 1917–1923*. Atglen, PA: Schiffer Publishing Ltd., 2008.

Dinnerstein, Leonard, Roger L. Nichols, and David M. Reimers. *Natives and Strangers: A Multicultural History of Americans*. New York: Oxford University Press, 1996.

Duffy, Francis P. *Father Duffy's Story*. New York: G. H. Doran, 1919.

Farwell, Byron. *Over There: The United States in the Great War, 1917–1918*. New York: W. W. Norton, 1999.

Faulkner, Richard S. *The School of Hard Knocks: Combat Leadership in the American Expeditionary Forces*. College Station: Texas A&M University Press, 2012.

Ferrell, Robert H. *Woodrow Wilson & World War I, 1917–1921*. New York: Harper & Row, 1985.

Fleming, Thomas. *The Illusion of Victory: America in World War I*. New York: Basic Books, 2003.

Ford, Nancy Gentile. *Americans All! Foreign-Born Soldiers in World War I*. College Station: Texas A&M University Press, 2001.

Fortescue, Major Granville. "Training the New Armies of Liberty." *National Geographic Magazine* 32, nos. 5–6 (November–December 1917): 421–437.

Harris, Stephen L. *Duffy's War*. Dulles, VA: Potomac Books, 2006.

Hoffman, Pvt. William R. *The Famous 42nd "Rainbow" Division Who Helped Close the Lid of Hell*. Plattsmouth, NE: Hoffman & Steinhauer, 1919.

Iorizzo, Luciano J., and Salvatore Mondello. *The Italian Americans*. New York: Twayne, 1971.

Johns, E. B. *Camp Travis and Its Part in the World War*. New York: E. B. Johns, 1919.

Johnson, Hugh S. *The Blue Eagle from Egg to Earth*. Garden City, NY: Doubleday, Doran, Inc, 1935.

Kennedy, David. *Over Here: The First World War and American Society*. Oxford: Oxford University Press, 1980.

Laskin, David. *The Long Way Home: An American Journey from Ellis Island to the Great War*. New York: Harper Collins, 2010.

Lebow, Eileen F. *A Grandstand Seat: The American Balloon Service in World War I*. Westport, CT: Praeger, 1998.

Lengel, Edward G. *To Conquer Hell: The Meuse Argonne, 1918*. New York: Henry Holt, 2008.

Liberty Loan Program Pamphlet. *What the War Will Do for America*. New York: Samuel Untermeyer, 1918.

Lonn, Ella. *Foreigners in the Union Army and Navy*. New York: Greenwood, 1969. Reprint of 1951 edition.

MacNider, Hanford. *The A.E.F. of a Conscientious Subaltern*. Illustrations by C. Leroy Baldridge. Mason City, IA: Klipto, 1924. Reprinted from *American Legion Weekly*, 1922–1923.

Magoffin, Ralph V. D. "Morale Work in an Army Camp." *Historical Outlook, Continuing the History Teacher's Magazine* 11, no. 2 (1920): 49.

March, General Peyton C. *The Nation at War*. Garden City, NY: Doubleday, Doran, 1932.

Mead, Gary. *The Doughboys: America and the First World War*. Woodstock, NY: Overlook, 2000.

Nenninger, Timothy K. "Tactical Dysfunction in the AEF, 1917–1918." *Military Affairs* 51, no. 4 (October 1987): 177–181. Published by the Department of History, Kansas State University.

Nugent, Walter. *Crossings: The Great Transatlantic Migrations, 1870–1914*. Bloomington: Indiana University Press, 1995.

Orlean, Susan. *Rin Tin Tin: The Life and the Legend*. New York: Simon & Schuster, 2011.

Pershing John J. *My Experiences in the World War*. Vol. 2. New York: Frederick A. Stokes, 1931.

Pershing, John J. *My Life before the World War, 1860–1917: A Memoir*. Edited by John T. Greenwood. Lexington, KY: University Press of Kentucky, 2013.

Powell, Maj. E. Alexander, USA. *The Army behind the Army*. New York: Charles Scribner's Sons, 1919.

Price, Raymond B. *Washington's Nine Months at War: Great Efforts—Disappointing Results—Why?* Washington, DC: Patriotic Education Society, December 1917.

Robinson, William J. *Forging the Sword: The Story of Camp Devens, New England's Army Cantonment*. Concord, NH: Rumford, 1920.

Rubin, Richard. *The Last of the Doughboys*. New York: Houghton Mifflin Harcourt, 2013.

Shay, Michael. *Sky Pilots: The Yankee Division Chaplains in World War I*. Columbia: University of Missouri Press, 2014.

Slotkin, Richard. *Lost Battalions*. New York: Henry Holt, 2005.

Stallings, Laurence T. *The Doughboys: The Story of the AEF, 1917–1918*. New York: Harper & Row, 1963.

Sterba, Christopher M. *Good Americans: Italian and Jewish Immigrants during the First World War*. New York: Oxford University Press, 2003.

Thisted, Moses N. *Pershing's Pioneer Infantry of World War I*. Hemet, CA: Alphabet Printers, 1981.

Wiley, Bell I., and Hirst D. Milhollen. *They Who Fought Here*. New York: Macmillan, 1959.

Woodward, David R. *The American Army and the First World War*. Armies of the Great War. Cambridge, UK: Cambridge University Press, 2014.

**Newspapers:**

*Camp Lee Bayonet*. Published in Petersburg, Virginia, 1917–1918.

*Evening Star*. Published in Washington, DC, 1917.

*Gas Attack*. The official magazine of the 27th Division. Published at Camp Wadsworth, SC, 1917–1918.

*The Indian*. The official news magazine of the 2nd Division. Published in the US Army Occupation Zone, 1919.

*New York Times*. Published in New York City, 1918–1922.

*Star and Stripes*. French edition, published in Paris, 1918–1919.

**Unit and Local Histories:**

Bach, Christian A., and Henry Noble Hall. *The Fourth Division: Its Services and Achievements in the World War*. Garden City, NY: Fourth Division, 1920.

Barber, J. Frank. *History of the Seventy-Ninth Division A.E.F. during the World War: 1917–1919*. Compiled and edited by the History Committee 79th Division Association, Lancaster, PA: Steinman & Steinman, Undated.

Burton, Harold H. *600 Days' Service: A History of the 361st Infantry Regiment of the United States Army*. Portland, OR: James, Kerns & Abbott, 1921.

Chastaine, Ben-Hur. *Story of the 36th: The Experiences of the 36th Division in the World War*. Oklahoma City, OK: Harlow, 1920.

City of Rochester. *World War Service Record of Rochester and Monroe County, New York*. Vol. 1, *Those Who Died for Us*. Rochester, NY: Du Bois, 1924.

Cole, Ralph D., and W. C. Howells. *The Thirty-Seventh Division in the World War, 1917–1918*. Vol. 1. Columbus, OH: Thirty-Seventh Veterans Association, 1926.

Commanding General 88th Division. *The 88th Division in the World War of 1914–1918*. New York: Wynkoop Hallenbeck Crawford, 1919.

Cutchins, John A. *History of the Twenty-Ninth Division "Blue and Gray," 1917–1919*. Philadelphia: McCalla, 1921.

Davis, Col. Abel, US Army. *The Story of the 132d Infantry, A.E.F.* (no publishing data, but probably Luxembourg, 1919), unpaginated.

Dienst, Capt. Charles F. *History of the 353rd Infantry Regiment, 89th Division National Army September 1917 to June 1919*. Wichita, KS: 353rd Infantry Society, 1921.

Divisional Officers. *Official History of 82nd Division American Expeditionary Forces, 1917–1919*. Indianapolis, IN: Bobbs-Merrill, 1920.

English, George H. *History of the 89th Division USA*. Denver, CO: War Society of the 89th Division, 1920.

Faribault County. *In the World War: Faribault County, Minnesota, 1917–1918–1919*. Wells, MI: Forum Advocate, undated.

Flint Daily Journal. *Honor Roll and Complete War History of Genesee County Michigan in the Great World War 1914 to 1918*. Flint, MI: Flint Daily Journal, 1920.

George, Albert E., and Captain Edwin H. Cooper. *Pictorial History of the Twenty-Sixth Division, United States Army*. Boston: Ball, 1920.

Goode, J. Roy. *The American Rainbow*. Self-published by J. Roy Goode, 1918.

Haight, Walter L. *Racine County in the World War*. Racine, WI: Western Printing & Lithographing, ca. 1920.

Huidekoper, Frederic Louis. *The History of the 33rd Division*. Vols. I–III. Springfield: Illinois State Historical Library, 1921.

Johnson, Harold S. *Roster of the Rainbow Division (Forty-Second)*. New York: Eaton & Gettinger, 1917.

Martin, Col. Edward. *The Twenty-Eighth Division in the World War*. 5 vols. Edited by E. S. Wallace. Pittsburgh, PA: 28th Division Publishing, 1924.

Reilly, Henry J. *Americans All: The Rainbow at War.* Columbus, OH: F. J. Heer, 1936.

Seal, Henry F. Jr. *History of the 116th U.S. Infantry Regiment 29th Infantry Division 1917–1919*. Richmond, VA: Private publishing by the Virginia Army National Guard, 1953.

77th Division Association. *History of the Seventy-Seventh Division, August 25th 1917–November 11th 1918*. New York: Wynkoop Hallenbeck Crawford, 1919.

Society of the Fifth Division. *The Fifth US Division in the World War, 1917–1919*. Washington, DC: Ouray Building, 1919.

Society of the First Division. *History of the First Division during the World War, 1917–1919*. Philadelphia: John C. Winston, 1922.

States Publication Society. *The Official History of the Eighty-Sixth Division*. Chicago: States Publication Society, 1921.

308th Engineers Veterans Association. *With the 308th Engineers from Ohio to the Rhine and Back*. Cleveland, OH: Premier, 1923.

353rd Infantry Regimental Society. *They're from Kansas: History of the 353rd Infantry Regiment, September 1917–June 1919*. Wichita, KS: Eagle, 1921.

Tiebout, Frank B. *A History of the 305th Infantry*. New York: Wynkoop Hallenbeck Crawford for the 305th Infantry Auxiliary, 1919.

29th Division Association. *The Twenty-Niner.* Frederick, MD: 29th Division Association, Quarterly.

Unknown. *A Short History and Illustrated Roster of 112th Infantry, Army of the United States*. Philadelphia: Edward Stern, 1918.

**Unpublished Sources:**

Belmonte, Peter L. "For Gallantry in Action: *Maranesi* Americans in World War I," unpublished paper based on research in Italian birth records, US draft, census, naturalization, and military records.

Brakebill, Max. Collection of letters while serving with the 40th Division, 1918–1919. Private collection.

Koehn, Robert. Collection of letters 1918–1919 from the 83rd Division. Private collection.

Keith, Wayne. Wartime diary of service in the States and in France with the 37th Division. Private Collection.

Simmons Public Library, Kenosha, Wisconsin. Typewritten list of Kenosha's World War I veterans, ca. 1936.

**Official Websites:**

Alvin York Institute, 701 North Main Street, Jamestown, TN 38556, home page: http//www2.
york.k12.tn.us.

American Battle Monuments Commission home page and website: http://www.abmc.gov.

Arlington National Cemetery official website: http://www.arlingtoncemetery.mil/.

Army National Guard home page and website: http://www.nationalguard.com/.

California State Military Museum home page and website: http://www.militarymuseum.org/
cpKearney2Photos.html/.

Camp Zachary Taylor Historical Society of Louisville, Kentucky, website: http://www.
camptaylorhistorical.org.

Congressional Medal Of Honor Society home page: http://www.cmohs.org.

State Archives of North Carolina and the North Carolina Digital Collections home page: http://
digital.ncdcr.gov/cdm/singleitem/collection/.

US Army Center for Military History website: http://www.history.army.mil/.

US Marine Corps History Division (USMC HD) website: https://www.mcu.usmc.mil/
historydivision/.

US Selective Service System website: https://www.sss.gov/About/History-And-Records/
Induction statistics.

West Point Association website: https://apps.westpointaog.org/Memorials/.

**Other Websites:**

Ancestry.com. Various archives and records.

The extract from "The Magpies in Picardy" by T. P. Cameron Wilson used in the dedication
is from *Up the Line to Death: The War Poets 1914–1918* by Brian Gardner (London:
Methuen, 1964).

**Photographs:**

All color photographs of the artifacts and uniforms, unless otherwise credited, are provided
courtesy of Alison Hutton.

A number of other included photographs and historical documents are courtesy of various
governmental, military, or historical organizations. Without their generosity, this work would
not be complete. These include:

Posters displayed on pages 17 and 21 are courtesy of the Library of Congress.

Special Collections & Archives Division, USMA Library

Library of Congress

National Archives

National Guard Educational Foundation

United States Special Operations Command (USASOC)

US Army Center for Military History (CMH)

US Army Military History Institute (USAMHI)

US Army Quartermaster Museum (USAQM)

US Marine Corps History Division (USMC HD)

Virginia National Guard Historical Collection

# INDEX